Tax Administration 2022

COMPARATIVE INFORMATION ON OECD AND OTHER ADVANCED AND EMERGING ECONOMIES

OECD

BETTER POLICIES FOR BETTER LIVES

This document, as well as any data and map included herein, are without prejudice to the status of or sovereignty over any territory, to the delimitation of international frontiers and boundaries and to the name of any territory, city or area.

The statistical data for Israel are supplied by and under the responsibility of the relevant Israeli authorities. The use of such data by the OECD is without prejudice to the status of the Golan Heights, East Jerusalem and Israeli settlements in the West Bank under the terms of international law.

Note by Turkey
The information in this document with reference to "Cyprus" relates to the southern part of the Island. There is no single authority representing both Turkish and Greek Cypriot people on the Island. Turkey recognises the Turkish Republic of Northern Cyprus (TRNC). Until a lasting and equitable solution is found within the context of the United Nations, Turkey shall preserve its position concerning the "Cyprus issue".

Note by all the European Union Member States of the OECD and the European Union
The Republic of Cyprus is recognised by all members of the United Nations with the exception of Turkey. The information in this document relates to the area under the effective control of the Government of the Republic of Cyprus.

Please cite this publication as:
OECD (2022), *Tax Administration 2022: Comparative Information on OECD and other Advanced and Emerging Economies*, OECD Publishing, Paris, https://doi.org/10.1787/1e797131-en.

ISBN 978-92-64-69704-1 (print)
ISBN 978-92-64-41168-5 (pdf)
ISBN 978-92-64-86659-1 (HTML)
ISBN 978-92-64-66895-9 (epub)

Tax Administration
ISSN 2308-7331 (print)
ISSN 2307-7727 (online)

Preface

The 2022 edition of the Tax Administration Series (TAS), like its predecessors, provides comparative information on the performance of advanced and emerging tax administrations globally and seeks to draw out the main underlying trends and challenges they face. The purpose and value of the TAS, first published in 2004, is to assist administrations, governments, taxpayers and other stakeholders in considering how and where improvements might be made in the efficiency and effectiveness of tax administration, including through learning from what others have done.

Looking outwards in this way has never been more important, as the world has changed in unforeseen ways over the past two years, bringing new challenges as well as new solutions. The COVID-19 pandemic has affected the lives of many people around the world, and governments have taken a wide range of actions to support their citizens and businesses during this difficult period

With this edition of the TAS containing data for fiscal years 2018 to 2020, we can very well see the fiscal impact of the pandemic - net revenue collection has declined while tax arrears have gone up significantly. The COVID-19 related changes in the operating models of tax administrations that have been observed in the previous edition, mainly based on examples and anecdotal evidence, are now underpinned with hard numbers. Many of the examples in this edition continue to showcase the agility, imagination and dedication of tax administrations and their staff in the ways that they supported taxpayers and wider government during the pandemic. We can also see how many administrations are now converting some of the emergency measures into business-as-usual, improving services to taxpayers, enhancing the efficiency and resiliency of tax administration systems and offering flexible working arrangements for staff.

This edition also continues to highlight the trend towards more digital services, which in many ways has accelerated as a result of the challenges faced during the COVID-19 pandemic. Leading a tax administration myself, it is clear to me that digital service delivery is going to be of central importance to us achieving our goals. Investing in leading-edge information technologies will strengthen our operational capabilities, including our agility in providing new services more frequently and adopting new technologies earlier, with the purpose of providing clients with a seamless digital service experience to help make the process of meeting tax obligations easier for taxpayers.

Finally, as Chair of the OECD Forum on Tax Administration and Commissioner of the Canada Revenue Agency, I would like to congratulate my own staff as well as my fellow Commissioners and their staff for their exceptional work over the challenging last 12 months.

I would also like to thank all those involved in producing this engaging and informative report, in particular Oliver Petzold and Paul Marsh of the OECD Secretariat. This edition of the TAS will help us all understand more about the challenges that we face individually and collectively. Through this, we can consider what we might do in our own jurisdictions but also identify where tax administrations can collaborate to improve our services to taxpayers across the globe.

Bob Hamilton

Chair of the OECD Forum on Tax Administration

Commissioner of the Canada Revenue Agency

Foreword

Tax Administration 2022 is the tenth edition of the OECD Centre for Tax Policy and Administration's comparative information series. First published in 2004, the primary purpose of the Tax Administration Series (TAS) is to share information that will facilitate dialogue on the design and administration of tax systems.

This edition of the TAS provides internationally comparative data on aspects of tax systems and their administration in 58 advanced and emerging economies. It includes performance-related data, ratios and trends up to the end of the 2020 fiscal year and, thus, provides a first glimpse at the impact of the COVID-19 pandemic on the work of tax administrations.

The publication also presents the results of the third and fourth round of the International Survey on Revenue Administration (ISORA). The ISORA survey is a multi-organisation survey to collect information and data on tax administration. It is governed by four partner organisations: the Inter-American Center of Tax Administrations (CIAT), the International Monetary Fund (IMF), the Intra-European Organisation of Tax Administrations (IOTA) and the OECD. As with the previous survey round, the Asian Development Bank (ADB) also participated in ISORA along with the four partner organisations.

To provide further insight into the ISORA data in certain places, TAS 2022 also uses data from the Inventory of Tax Technology Initiatives (ITTI). ITTI is a new online database containing information on technology tools and digitalisation solutions implemented by tax administrations across the globe. It has been developed by the OECD's Forum on Tax Administration together with eight key partner organisations.

This report was approved by the Committee on Fiscal Affairs on 11 May 2022 and prepared for publication by the OECD Secretariat.

Acknowledgements

The OECD has produced the Tax Administration Series, its comparative information series on tax administration, since 2004. Since that time the publication has grown in terms of its coverage, influence and importance and is now widely recognised as an authoritative source of information on tax administration around the globe.

The 2022 Tax Administration publication presents the results of the third and fourth round of the International Survey on Revenue Administration (ISORA) which were launched in September 2020 and September 2021, respectively. It would not have been possible without the direct support and help of a large number of people, particularly the staff in the 58 tax administrations that provided data and jurisdiction examples, reviewed content and responded to feedback and questions on the data and text that form the basis of the publication.

The principal authors of the publication were Paul Marsh and Oliver Petzold both Advisors in the OECD's Forum on Tax Administration (FTA) Secretariat. Management and analysis of the ISORA data was undertaken by Oliver Petzold and Vegard Holmedahl, also an Advisor in the FTA Secretariat. Authoring support was provided by Peter Green, Head of the FTA Secretariat. The authors are also thankful to Raffaele Articolo, also from the FTA Secretariat, for his assistance in the production of the publication.

Finally, the authors would like to thank the work of the wider team at the OECD Secretariat, in particular Sonia Nicolas, Eunkyung Shin and Jose Puig Pimentel, and the OECD Centre for Tax Policy and Administration's Communications team, in particular Carrie Tyler, Natalie Lagorce, Hazel Healy and Karena Garnier.

Table of contents

FIGURES

TABLES

BOXES

Follow OECD Publications on:

 *http://twitter.com/OECD_Pubs*

http://www.facebook.com/OECDPublications

http://www.linkedin.com/groups/OECD-Publications-4645871

http://www.youtube.com/oecdilibrary

http://www.oecd.org/oecddirect/

This book has...

A service that delivers Excel® files from the printed page!

Look for the *StatLink* at the bottom of the tables or graphs in this book. To download the matching Excel® spreadsheet, just type the link into your Internet browser or click on the link from the digital version.

Reader's guide

Tax Administrations covered by the report

Tax Administration 2022 is the tenth edition of the OECD Centre for Tax Policy and Administration's comparative Tax Administration Series (TAS). The primary purpose of the series, which commenced in 2004, is to share information that will facilitate dialogue among tax officials on important tax administration issues, and to identify opportunities to improve the design and administration of their systems.

This edition of the series provides internationally comparative data on various aspects of tax systems and their administration in 58 advanced and emerging economies. It covers 52 jurisdictions that are members of the OECD's Forum on Tax Administration (FTA). In addition, it includes information on the non-FTA jurisdictions that are members of the European Union (i.e. Bulgaria, Croatia, Cyprus, and Malta) as well as Morocco and Thailand (which increases the report's geographical coverage).

ISORA data gathering process and reporting

The publication presents the results of the third and fourth round of the International Survey on Revenue Administration (ISORA) which were launched in September 2020 and September 2021, respectively. The ISORA survey is a multi-organisation international survey that collects national-level information and data on tax administration. It is governed by four partner organisations: the Inter-American Center of Tax Administrations (CIAT), the International Monetary Fund (IMF), the Intra-European Organisation of Tax Administrations (IOTA) and the OECD. Since the 2018 ISORA survey round, the Asian Development Bank (ADB) also participates in ISORA along with the four partner organisations.

2020 changes to the ISORA structure and process

Following the completion of the 2018 ISORA survey, the ISORA partners reviewed the data produced by the survey, and engaged with participating administrations to gather feedback on the survey process.

The review showed that some questions suffered from a low response rate, and that the quality of the responses was mixed in some areas. Administrations confirmed that the data was useful for international comparison, for preparation of missions to other jurisdictions and for briefing documents. They did note that the survey process was complex and time consuming, and that it was desirable for the data to be timelier.

Considering this, the ISORA partners agreed that there was a need for a major revision before launching ISORA 2020, in order to reduce burdens on tax administrations in completing the survey and to improve the quality of responses. The survey review determined that responses to many questions would remain unchanged between years, thus opening the opportunity for splitting the ISORA survey into two parts:

1. **Questions to be asked in an annual ISORA survey**. These questions mainly focus on the operational performance of tax administrations, allowing the annual survey to be significantly

reduced in size and making it easier to complete. This also allows data to be made available more quickly to participating administrations. The 2020 and 2021 ISORA surveys fall in this category.

2. ***Questions to be asked every four-five years.*** These are mainly questions where responses are less likely to change between survey iterations. A significant number of questions included in the 2016 and 2018 ISORA surveys would fall within this category. Understanding that responses to those questions are more likely to remain stable over a longer period, means they need to be asked less frequently, thus reducing administration's annual burden of completing the survey. The ISORA partners are still in the process of designing this supplementary ISORA survey which is intended to be launched in 2023.

Survey management

The 2020 and 2021 ISORA surveys collected data for fiscal years 2018, 2019 and 2020. Survey information was gathered online using the IMF's Revenue Administration Fiscal Information Tool (RA-FIT). Participation was voluntary and more than 150 administrations completed the survey. Each partner organisation, and the ADB, supported participants by assisting them with the completion of the ISORA survey, based on an upfront agreed allocation key. The 58 administrations included in this publication corresponds to the group of administrations supported by the OECD.

While all data contained in the publication has been subject to a high-level review by the OECD, neither the OECD nor any other partner organisation formally validated the data. As a result, all data included in the publication should be considered as self-reported by the administrations concerned.

Data available to the public

Historically, the OECD makes all ISORA data for TAS participants publicly available through the TAS and its data annex. Similarly, the ADB publishes jurisdiction-level ISORA data for its members. See, for example, its publication *A Comparative Analysis of Tax Administration in Asia and the Pacific 2020 Edition* (Asian Development Bank, 2020[1]). The other ISORA partners, do the following:

- IMF publishes in aggregated form. See, for example, the IMF publication *ISORA 2018: Understanding Revenue Administration* (Crandall, Gavin and Masters, 2021[2]); and

- CIAT publishes selected data points. See, for example, the CIAT publication *Overview of Tax Administrations: structure; income, resources and personnel; operation and digitalization: ISORA* (Díaz de Sarralde, 2019[3]).

In addition, starting with the 2020 ISORA survey, all ISORA data is made available to the public on the RA-FIT data portal (https://data.rafit.org/).

Data comparability

TAS 2022 includes performance-related data, ratios and other information for the fiscal years 2018, 2019 and 2020. The 2018 and 2019 data was collected through the 2020 ISORA survey and already included in TAS 2021. However, a number of administrations updated some of their 2018 and 2019 data during the process of producing the 2022 edition of the TAS. For that reason, there might be some differences between TAS 2021 and 2022 figures and tables displaying 2018 and 2019 data.

In certain areas, TAS 2022 also uses data from the 2016 and 2018 ISORA rounds to show trends for the period between 2014 and 2020. However, as noted above, the changes in the ISORA process meant that the ISORA 2020 and 2021 surveys have been reduced significantly in size when compared to the 2016 and 2018 version. In addition, following the review, a number of changes were made to questions to improve clarity and data quality. Therefore, care needs to be taken when comparing results from ISORA 2020 and 2021 with ISORA 2016 and 2018, and the wording of survey questions compared whenever relevant. The survey questions can be accessed on https://data.rafit.org/ under "Forms and Guides" in the section "Publication/Links".

As a result of the changes to the ISORA survey, TAS 2022 may not comment on certain data points that were covered in the 2019 edition of the TAS (OECD, 2019[4]). For those data points, the 2019 edition remains the most recent source.

Also, it should be noted that statistical data is often subject to revisions after publication. As a result, some data may not correspond to what has been published by administrations. For example, it may be that opening balances of a specific year (t) may not correspond to closing balances of the preceding year (t-1) that were published in earlier editions of this publication.

Even more care should be taken when comparing ISORA data with data gathered through pre-ISORA surveys, i.e. data included in the sixth and prior editions of the TAS. When the ISORA survey was initially created and at the request of survey participants, the four partner organisations made considerable effort to agree and document a range of words and terms used in the survey and their meaning. While this has improved data integrity and comparability between administrations, comparisons with pre-ISORA data may be limited as definitions may now exist for terms not previously defined, or in some instances, have changed.

Further, in relation to combined tax and customs administrations, it should be noted that the data in this publication refers to the tax administration activities of such administrations. The data may therefore not be directly comparable with key performance indicators published by them as these indicators may include both tax and customs related data.

Data from the Inventory of Tax Technology Initiatives

To complement the ISORA survey data, this edition of the TAS also uses data from the Inventory of Tax Technology Initiatives (ITTI) which contains information on technology tools and digitalisation solutions implemented by more than 75 tax administrations. It has been put together with the assistance of the ISORA partners, the ADB, the African Tax Administration Forum, the *Cercle de Reflexion et d'Echange des Dirigeants des Administrations Fiscale*, the Commonwealth Association of Tax Administrators and the Study Group on Asia-Pacific Tax Administration and Research. (OECD, 2022[5])

The inventory data is collected through a global survey on digitalisation, and can offer further insight into the ISORA data in certain places. Therefore, where available, this edition of the TAS uses the ITTI data from 52 out of the 58 tax administrations that are covered in this report and that have completed the global survey on digitalisation.

Publication structure

The series examines the fundamental elements of modern tax administration systems and uses data analysis and examples supplied by tax administrations to highlight key trends, recent innovations, and performance measures and indicators.

Structure

The main body of the publication is structured around nine chapters: (i) an introduction followed by chapters on (ii) responsibilities and revenue collections; (iii) registration and identification; (iv) assessment; (v) services; (vi) verification and compliance management; (vii) collection; (viii) disputes; and (ix) budget and workforce.

The publication also contains two annexes:

- Annex A contains the tables with the ISORA 2020 and 2021 survey responses provided by tax administrations[1] which form the basis of the analysis in this report:
  - The first set of tables contains a number of indicators derived from the data submitted via the ISORA survey (tables starting with "D"). The formulae and data points used for calculating the indicators are shown below each of these tables.
  - The second set of tables contains the raw ISORA 2020 and 2021 survey data. Those are the tables starting with "A".
  - The last two tables holds external data points that were used to calculate some of the D-table indicators. Those tables start with "E".
- Annex B has the details of the administrations that participated in this publication.

Both annexes are visible online only and can be viewed here: https://doi.org/10.1787/1e797131-en.

Tables and figures

The tables and figures in the publication are all accompanied by hyperlinks (OECD StatLinks) that direct readers to corresponding MS Excel spreadsheets containing the underlying data. These links are stable and will remain unchanged over time.

Typically, the source notes below the figures in the main body of the publication refers readers to the underlying data that is contained in Annex A. In some cases, they may refer to previous editions of the TAS or, where ITTI data is used, to the relevant MS Excel spreadsheets on ITTI.

Symbols and abbreviations that are used in the data tables are explained at the bottom of each table. The reader should note that where no data is shown for a specific jurisdiction in a table this is primarily due to the question not being applicable to a particular jurisdiction, or an opening question to a sub-section of the survey being answered in the negative and, therefore, the jurisdiction did not have to answer the follow-up questions.

Forum on Tax Administration

The FTA is a unique body bringing together tax commissioners from over 50 advanced and emerging economies from across the globe. Readers wishing to find out more about the OECD's work on tax administration should go to www.oecd.org/tax/forum-on-tax-administration/.

Caveat

Tax administrations operate in varied environments, and the way in which they each administer their taxation system differs in respect to their policy and legislative environment and their administrative practice and culture. As such, a standard approach to tax administration may be neither practical nor desirable in a particular instance. Therefore, this report and the observations it makes need to be interpreted with this in mind. Care should be taken when considering a jurisdiction's practices to fully appreciate the complex factors that have shaped a particular approach. Similarly, regard needs to be had to the distinct challenges and priorities each administration is managing.

Notes

[1] For Japan, given that it publishes its currency figures in millions the currency figures included in tables have had added a suffix of "000" in order to fit the survey requirements that currency figures needed to be provided in thousands.

References

Asian Development Bank (2020), *A Comparative Analysis of Tax Administration in Asia and the Pacific: 2020 Edition*, Asian Development Bank, Manila, https://doi.org/10.22617/TCS190240. [1]

Crandall, W., E. Gavin and A. Masters (2021), *ISORA 2018: Understanding Revenue Administration*, International Monetary Fund, Washington, DC, https://www.imf.org/en/Publications/Departmental-Papers-Policy-Papers/Issues/2021/11/03/Understanding-Revenue-Administration-464865 (accessed on 13 May 2022). [2]

Díaz de Sarralde, S. (2019), *Overview of Tax Administrations: structure; income, resources and personnel; operation and digitalization. ISORA*, Inter-American Center of Tax Administrations (CIAT), Panama City, https://www.ciat.org/Biblioteca/Estudios/2019_Overview_AT-ISORA_sarralde.pdf (accessed on 13 May 2022). [3]

OECD (2022), *Inventory of Tax Technology Initiatives*, https://www.oecd.org/tax/forum-on-tax-administration/tax-technology-tools-and-digital-solutions/ (accessed on 13 May 2022). [5]

OECD (2019), *Tax Administration 2019: Comparative Information on OECD and other Advanced and Emerging Economies*, OECD Publishing, Paris, https://doi.org/10.1787/74d162b6-en. [4]

Abbreviations and acronyms

ADB	Asian Development Bank
AEAT	Agencia Estatal de Administración Tributaria (Spain)
AEOI	Automatic Exchange of Information
AFIP	Administración Federal de Ingresos Públicos (Argentina)
AI	Artificial Intelligence
AIS	Annual Information Statement
APA	Advance Pricing Agreement
API	Application Programming Interface
AT	Autoridade Tributária e Aduaneira (Portugal)
ATO	Australian Taxation Office
ATR	Additional Tax Revenue
AUD	Australian Dollar
BAS	Business Activity Statement
BC	British Columbia
BEPS	Base Erosion and Profit Shifting
BMF	Bundesministerium für Finanzen (Austria)
BNRA	Bulgarian National Revenue Agency
BRL	Brazilian Reals
CAD	Canadian Dollar
CIAT	Inter-American Center of Tax Administrations
CIT	Corporate Income Tax
COP	Colombian Peso
COTS	Commercial-Off-The-Shelf
CRA	Canada Revenue Agency
CRS	Common Reporting Standard
CSP	Credential Service Provider
CTC	Child Tax Credit

DFA	Digital Financial Asset
DGFiP	Direction Générale des Finances Publiques (France)
DGT	Directorate General of Taxes (Indonesia)
DIAN	Dirección de Impuestos y Aduanas Nacionales (Colombia)
DSP	Digital Service Provider
ED	Department of Education (United States)
eIDAS	Electronic Identification Authentication and Trust Services
ETCB	Estonian Tax and Customs Board
EU	European Union
EUR	Euro
FATCA	Foreign Account Tax Compliance Act
FEDR	Fixed Expenses Deduction Ratio
FTA	Forum on Tax Administration
FTE	Full Time Equivalent
FY	Fiscal Year
GBP	Great Britain Pound
GDP	Gross Domestic Product
GRS	Georgia Revenue Service
GST/HST	Goods and Services Tax / Harmonized Sales Tax
HMRC	Her Majesty's Revenue and Customs (United Kingdom)
HNWI	High Net Wealth Individual
ICAP	International Compliance Assurance Programme
ICT	Information and Communication Technology
IEC	Integrated E-Filing and Centralized Processing Centre
IGN	Institut national de l'information géographique et forestière (France)
IMF	International Monetary Fund
IOTA	Intra-European Organisation of Tax Administrations
IRA	Italian Revenue Agency
IRS	Internal Revenue Service (United States)
IRAS	Inland Revenue Authority of Singapore
IRBM	Inland Revenue Board of Malaysia
ISORA	International Survey on Revenue Administration
IT	Information Technology
ITA	Israel Tax Authority
ITTI	Inventory of Tax Technology Initiatives

KRA	Kenya Revenue Authority
LB&I	Large Business and International
LTO/P	Large Taxpayer Office/Programme
MAP	Mutual Agreement Procedure
MBR	Modernising Business Registers
MFA	Multi-factor Authentication
MNE	Multinational Enterprise
MTD	Making Tax Digital
MVP	Minimum Viable Products
NAFA	National Agency for Fiscal Administration (Romania)
NFS	No-Filing Service
NRC	Número de Referencia completo (Full Reference Number)
NTA	National Tax Agency (Japan)
NTA	Norwegian Tax Administration
NTA	Netherlands Tax Administration
NTCA	National Tax and Customs Administration (Hungary)
NZD	New Zealand Dollar
ODSS	Optimising Disputes through Self-Service
OECD	Organisation for Economic Co-operation and Development
PAYE	Pay-As-You-Earn
PCG	Passcode Grid
PIT	Personal Income Tax
RA-FIT	Revenue Administration Fiscal Information Tool
RFB	Receita Federal do Brasil
RPA	Robotic Process Automation
SA	Self Assessment
SADI	Secure Access Digital Identity
SEK	Swedish krona
SII	Servicio de Impuestos Internos (Chile)
SMS	Short Message Service
SSC	Social Security Contribution
SPID	Sistema Pubblico di Identità Digitale (Public Digital Identity System)
SSI	Self Sovereign Identity
STA	State Taxation Administration (People's Republic of China)
STA	Swedish Tax Administration

STI	State Tax Inspectorate (Lithuania)
SUNAT	Superintendencia Nacional de Aduanas y de Administración Tributaria (Peru)
TAS	Tax Administration Series
UK	United Kingdom
US	United States
USD	United States Dollar
VAT	Value Added Tax
VICA	Virtual Intelligent Chat Assistant
WHT	Withholding Tax

Executive summary

With the participation of 58 jurisdictions accounting for around 90% of global GDP, the tenth edition of the OECD's Tax Administration Series (TAS 2022) provides a comprehensive view of the state of tax administration in 2020. The report, which provides comparative information in 76 tables covering tax administration performance and profile data, is intended to assist tax administrations in consideration of where further improvements might be made, as well to enhance wider public understanding as to the scale and the changing nature of global tax administration. This 2022 edition also attempts to draw out, from both the data provided through the International Survey of Revenue Administrations (ISORA) and the more than 100 examples received from over 35 tax administrations, the most significant changes that tax administrations are dealing with. It focuses in particular on how tax administrations are increasingly looking at the opportunities to take more proactive approaches to influencing and managing compliance as well as the challenges they face in adapting to the changing resource requirements.

Table 1. Key figures related to the tax administrations covered in this publication

Staff employed	1 700 000
Audits/verifications	20 000 000
In-person enquiries	54 000 000
Telephone calls received	330 000 000
Number of active PIT and CIT taxpayers	865 000 000
Contacts via online taxpayer account	1 310 000 000
Number of tax returns (PIT, CIT and VAT) received	1 370 000 000
Operational budget (in EUR)	79 000 000 000
Collectable arrears at year-end (in EUR)	900 000 000 000
Total arrears at year-end (in EUR)	2 310 000 000 000
Net revenue collected (in EUR)	12 070 000 000 000

Note: The figures are based on data obtained through the 2020 and 2021 ISORA surveys. The data has been converted to EUR using the exchange rate of 31 March 2022. They are minimum figures as not all administrations were able to provide information for all data points. Figures typically relate to the fiscal year 2020. Data for fiscal year 2019 was used where 2020 data was not available.

To complement the ISORA survey data, this edition of the TAS also uses data from the recently launched Inventory of Tax Technology Initiatives (ITTI) (OECD, 2022[1]) which contains information on technology tools and digitalisation solutions implemented by more than 75 tax administrations. The inventory data is collected through a global survey on digitalisation, and offers additional insight into the ISORA data on certain topics.

Impact of the COVID-19 pandemic

This is the first edition of the TAS that shows the impact of the COVID-19 pandemic on tax administrations. Figure 1 below highlights how the pandemic has had a significant impact on net revenue and tax arrears.

Tracking these indicators will be of great interest in future editions of this series, to see if, and how quickly they bounce back.

The COVID-19 pandemic fundamentally challenged the operating models of tax administrations, and it saw some significant changes in the way they interacted with taxpayers, with for example a drop of 55% in in-person visits, and a 30% increase in digital contacts. Tax administrations have proved to be resilient in the face of these challenges, and, as the examples in this edition show, they have continued to innovate and to deliver high quality services to taxpayers. In parallel, many tax administrations took on new services as part of wider government COVID-19 support schemes. This may be an acceleration of the trend noted in earlier editions of the TAS for administrations to take on new responsibilities, reflecting the deep expertise of tax administrations in delivering services to taxpayers, and in handling large and complex data sets.

The innovations highlighted in this edition of the report also show how the pandemic accelerated the growth in digital services and digital transformation and led to the consideration of new ways of working more generally. Many tax administrations report that they are now reflecting on their experiences during the pandemic and considering what this means for future tax administration, including for employees as well as taxpayers.

Figure 1. COVID-19 impact on tax administration

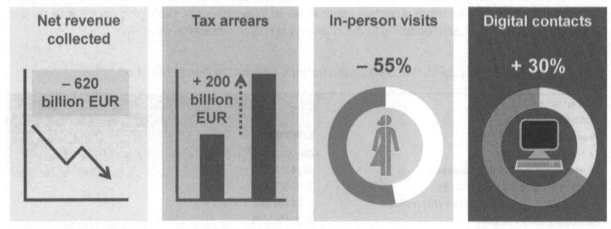

Note: The figures are based on data obtained through the 2020 and 2021 ISORA surveys. The data has been converted to EUR using the exchange rate of 31 March 2022.

Moving towards digital transformation

Previous editions of the TAS have shown a significant trend towards **e-administration** with an increasing uptake of online filing of tax returns as well as online payments and, in many jurisdictions, a move towards the full or partial prefilling of tax returns. This 2022 edition shows how that trend has continued and been accelerated by the pandemic, with digital contact channels now dominating interactions with taxpayers. For example, tax administrations reported that in 2020 there were around 1.3 billion contacts via online taxpayer accounts – an annual growth of 27%.

This report also highlights how tax administrations are starting to move towards **digital transformation**, with Figure 2 highlighting that around 75% of administrations have a digital transformation strategy in place.

Figure 2. Existence of a strategy for digital transformation in tax administrations, 2022

Percent of administrations

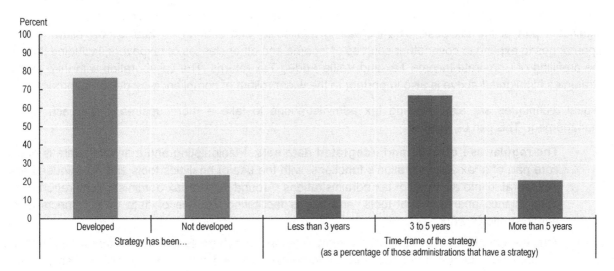

Note: The figure is based on ITTI data from 52 jurisdictions that are covered in this report and that have completed the global survey on digitalisation.
Source: (OECD et al. (2022), Inventory of Tax Technology Initiatives, https://www.oecd.org/tax/forum-on-tax-administration/tax-technology-tools-and-digital-solutions/, Table SG1 (accessed on 13 May 2022).

StatLink ᛑᛁᛋᛚ https://doi.org/10.1787/888934310385

Tax administrations report that these strategies are driving their digital services to become 'smarter', allowing taxpayers to complete increasingly complex tasks digitally, more efficiently and 24/7. This is also helping to bring important improvements in taxpayer compliance, and there are growing signs that the pace of digital transformation will accelerate further. This edition of the TAS highlights two broad themes in the drive towards digital transformation: engaging with taxpayers and compliance management.

Engaging with taxpayers

With more and more services being delivered online, the ways tax administrations engage with taxpayers is evolving. Effective digital engagement is being driven by two main factors:

- **Secure digital identity and verification**: As tax administrations deliver more and more of their services online, digital security, digital verification and digital identity is becoming the cornerstone of tax administrations' work. Tax administrations are leveraging their expertise and data sets to not only give taxpayers greater self-service access to tax administration services, but also to third parties and to wider government systems. Common digital identities are critical to these programmes.

- **Collaboration with third party service providers**: Embedding services and processes in the natural systems used by taxpayers in their daily lives and businesses is a growing trend among tax administrations. While this helps to improve tax compliance, it also reduces administrative burdens and frees up time that owners can use to grow their businesses. As these forms of collaboration become more common and sophisticated, tax administrations are starting to take strategic approaches to managing and providing support to service providers. This can include co-creation activities, as well as allowing direct data exchanges through Application Programming Interfaces (APIs).

Compliance management

Compliance-by-design approaches have been in place for many years for salaried personal income taxpayers through Pay-As-You-Earn withholding and reporting by employers. These systemic arrangements, adopted by almost all tax administrations, have helped maximise compliance for this significant part of the tax base. The increasing availability and sharing of data is now allowing such approaches to expand to cover other sources of income and other classes of taxpayers, including through the prefilling of Corporate Income Tax and Value Added Tax returns. The collaboration with third parties strategies highlighted above is also important to the wider rollout of compliance-by-design approaches.

Digital techniques are also allowing tax administrations to take a more upstream approach to risk management. This can be seen in:

- **The regular use of large and integrated data sets**. Manipulating and managing data is now a core part of a tax administration's functions, with the use of analytics tools and techniques being incorporated into all areas of tax administrations. Around 90% of tax administrations report using data science and analytical tools, and this is facilitating the use of data in all aspects of an administration's work.

- **The increasing use of artificial intelligence and machine learning**. As tax administrations become more comfortable with managing large data sets and computing power increases, the use of artificial intelligence and machine learning is opening up new approaches in risk management. Figure 3 highlights that over 70% of tax administrations report that they are already using cutting-edge techniques to exploit data in ways that can uncover previously hidden assets or identify new risks.

Figure 3. Use of data analytics in tax administrations, 2022

Percent of administrations

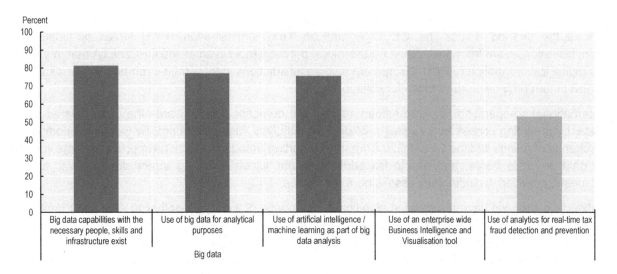

Note: The figure is based on ITTI data from 52 jurisdictions that are covered in this report and that have completed the global survey on digitalisation

Source: OECD et al (2022), Inventory of Tax Technology Initiatives, https://www.oecd.org/tax/forum-on-tax-administration/tax-technology-tools-and-digital-solutions/, Table DM5 (accessed on 13 May 2022).

StatLink 🖳 https://doi.org/10.1787/888934310404

Tax administration resources

Budgetary constraints continue to impact tax administrations. While the majority of administrations report increasing operational expenditures in absolute terms, this may not show the whole picture, as administrations are dealing with increased responsibilities, the pressures of technology change and the changing structure of their workforce. There is also significant variation in the amount of operational and capital expenditure on information and communication technology. While this may often be due to different sourcing and business approaches, it also raises the question as to whether expenditure levels in some cases may be somewhat low to support the demands for more sophisticated services, the ongoing digital transformation of tax administrations as well as enhancing resilience to respond to future crises.

Technology is helping tax administrations respond to these budgetary challenges, and an emerging trend that is showing remarkable results, is the growing use of Robotic Process Automation (RPA), where machines are used to complete repetitive tasks. Tax administration examples contributed to this report have highlighted that RPA is not only significantly increasing operational efficiency, but employee satisfaction is increasing as they can focus on the more interesting, challenging tasks.

One of the biggest shifts caused by the pandemic was the growth in remote working, and tax administrations are now considering how they adjust their working practices to take advantage of the benefits that can be offered from more flexible working arrangements. Digital transformation is also proving central to the shift towards longer-term remote working. As the examples show, it is being used in HR processes such as staff recruitment, staff training and performance management to help maintain the performance levels within administrations, and be ready for the challenges ahead.

International co-operation

Supporting much of the work of tax administrations is the continuing growth in the scale and scope of international co-operation, and the sharing of knowledge between tax administrations has never been more important as jurisdictions implement significant changes. This report forms part of that programme of knowledge sharing across the OECD Forum on Tax Administration (FTA) which is helping tax administrations learn from each other. Furthermore, practical tools such as the OECD FTA maturity model on digital transformation (OECD, 2021[2]) are helping jurisdictions identify their strengths and weaknesses, which in turn provides further focus for collaboration.

International co-operation has also helped support the domestic trend towards the sophisticated use of data, by providing access to data sets provided by initiatives such as Country-by-Country reporting, the exchange of rulings and the OECD/G20 Common Reporting Standard. These have provided large volumes of data on cross border activities to tax administrations, which is adding a new dimension to existing domestic activities, including risk assessment processes.

Tax administrations have also gained significant experience of working together to effectively implement complex international initiatives such as the OECD/G20 BEPS Package, and the OECD's multilateral International Compliance Assurance Programme, where taxpayers and tax administrations work co-operatively and multilaterally in close to real-time to undertake risk assessment and assurance of key international tax risks. As tax administrations go through their own processes of digital transformation, the next challenge will be how that domestic learning can be applied across borders, to use the new technology to support real-time cross-border exchange of information and to provide more seamless outcomes for taxpayers as well as early tax certainty. This may offer opportunities to help ensure the effective and efficiency implementation of new initiatives such as the 'Two-Pillar Solution to Address the Tax Challenges Arising from the Digitalisation of the Economy' (OECD, 2021[3]).

References

OECD (2022), *Inventory of Tax Technology Initiatives*, https://www.oecd.org/tax/forum-on-tax-administration/tax-technology-tools-and-digital-solutions/ (accessed on 13 May 2022). [1]

OECD (2021), *Digital Transformation Maturity Model*, OECD, Paris, https://www.oecd.org/tax/forum-on-tax-administration/publications-and-products/digital-transformation-maturity-model.htm (accessed on 13 May 2022). [2]

OECD (2021), *Statement on a Two-Pillar Solution to Address the Tax Challenges Arising from the Digitalisation of the Economy, OECD/G20 Base Erosion and Profit Shifting Project, 8 October 2021*, https://www.oecd.org/tax/beps/statement-on-a-two-pillar-solution-to-address-the-tax-challenges-arising-from-the-digitalisation-of-the-economy-october-2021.pdf (accessed on 13 May 2022). [3]

1 Introduction

This chapter provides an overview of the content of the 2022 edition of the OECD's Tax Administration Series.

Previous editions of the OECD's Tax Administration Series (TAS) have set out how, over time, tax administrations have evolved to respond to the changing environment in which they operate. This 2022 edition continues to track that evolution, and provides further insight into how tax administrations are:

- Enhancing their technological capabilities to deliver new ways of serving their customers;
- Becoming more collaborative and integrated with wider government;
- Building their skills in Artificial Intelligence and embedding it into their working practices
- Creating new compliance management techniques; and
- Enhancing their collection capabilities.

This edition of the TAS is also the first to reflect the impact of the COVID-19 pandemic. As could be expected, the scale and the speed of evolution of the crisis challenged the established systems and processes of tax administrations globally and had significant fiscal impacts, which this edition starts to show.

The pandemic however has also provided a catalyst for change within tax administrations. They have had to adapt to new ways of working both within the administration and in their interactions with taxpayers. Throughout this edition of the TAS, there are statistics and examples that show both the impact of the pandemic and the rapid innovations undertaken by tax administrations in response, many of which may persist in the longer-term.

The resilience and adaptability of tax administrations witnessed during the crisis have been facilitated and enabled by the wider technological changes taking place across the economy, including the expansion of social media, mobile platforms, cloud computing, big data technologies and advanced analytics techniques. These changes are creating new opportunities for tax administrations, citizens and businesses.

It is likely that these changes will be a recurring theme through future editions of the TAS, as tax administrations around the globe respond to the ongoing digitalisation of the economy, implementing new digital technologies to enhance taxpayer service quality, reduce operational and compliance burdens and increase revenues. In addition to the ongoing incremental improvement of the current system of tax administration, the journey towards a more fundamental change in the nature of tax administration is becoming clearer. This concerns a more system-wide compliance management approach in which tax administrations try to closely engage with the evolving natural systems that taxpayers use to manage their business, undertake transactions and communicate in order to reduce errors, minimise burdens and increasingly build-in tax compliance.

It is already possible to see many tax administrations taking advantage of new opportunities to administer taxes, support taxpayers and enhance compliance, enabled by the new technologies and tools. In particular, many tax administrations are making greater use of machine learning and artificial intelligence to deliver new compliance approaches. Tax administrations are also starting to explore how technology can 'embed' tax administration processes, traditionally carried out within the tax administration's own systems, into the services that third parties, such as software suppliers, provide to taxpayers. Partnerships and collaborations in this way can help improve the service provided to taxpayers and allow tax compliance to be increasingly moved upstream, closer to taxable transactions, helping to build in compliance and reduce burdens.

These changes can be seen in the data collected through the 2021 version of the International Survey on Revenue Administration (ISORA). Alongside the survey, the tax administrations covered in the TAS were also invited to provide examples of innovative practices that they are undertaking to help achieve their objectives. They have provided a rich source of over 100 examples, covering a wide range of topics. While these examples do not form a basis for comparison across tax administrations in the same way as the ISORA data points can, they do add more colour to the data, and tell a forward-looking story of the strategic direction of travel of tax administration. Furthermore, this edition of the TAS also contains some data points from the Inventory of Tax Technology Initiatives (ITTI) (OECD, 2022[1]). ITTI collects data on the digital transformation and digitalisation work of 76 tax administrations from across the globe, and this rich new source of data can provide further insight into the developments taking place in tax administration, facilitating mutual learning and collaboration.

Regardless of the wider shifts in the nature of tax administration, the core objectives of a tax administration remain the same, namely the timely and accurate collection of tax revenues to fund public services. *Chapter 2* explores this topic in more detail, and provides statistics on the range and value of taxes that administrations are responsible for.

Central to effective collection is the work of tax administrations to ensure that all relevant taxpayers are registered and can be identified, as necessary, both quickly and securely. *Chapter 3* sets out the work of tax administrations in this field, and also shows how this expertise is increasingly being leveraged to support wider governmental objectives on digital identity.

Chapter 4 looks at the tax assessment function, which includes all activities related to processing tax returns and payments. This chapter examines the use of e-channels for filing and paying, and outlines administrations' efforts to provide pre-filled returns, and the levels of on-time return filing and payment.

A common theme in this edition of the TAS is how tax administrations are becoming increasingly proactive in their management of the compliance environment, using the data generated by digitalisation to obtain new insights on compliance issues and treatments, and to use it as the basis for innovative solutions to existing problems.

Chapter 5 highlights how tax administrations are using sophisticated technological approaches to encourage 'self-service' by taxpayers. This is part of a more fundamental change whereby tax administration becomes a seamless process, with non-compliance and administrative burdens increasingly "designed out". *Chapter 6* explores this further and picks out how compliance approaches are changing, with the use of data and new technology tools to identify and take targeted enforcement action against those who fail to meet their obligations.

Chapter 7 explores how tax administrations manage the collection of outstanding debt, and examines the features of a modern tax debt collection function. These functions are essential to maintaining high levels of voluntary compliance and citizens' confidence in the overall tax system. This chapter also provides examples of approaches applied by administrations to minimise or even prevent debt being incurred. However, inevitably, disputes between taxpayers and tax administrations do arise, and *Chapter 8* considers those processes that safeguard taxpayer rights and ensure appropriate checks and balances exist on the exercising of tax powers by administrations.

Underpinning all of this work are the resources that are devoted to tax administrations, including their highly dedicated workforce. *Chapter 9* provides information on the resources that tax administrations have at their disposal, and picks out a number of trends that can be observed in the data over time. It also sets out the challenges administrations are managing in increasing their capability while managing a workforce that in general terms is reducing in size and on average is getting older. These challenges have been compounded by the pressures of the pandemic, and this chapter begins to consider the longer-term impact of those pressures. This is also an area where technology has an important role to play in helping to ensure that tax administrations and their staff are able to respond effectively to future challenges, in particular the digital transformation of the wider economy.

Reference

OECD (2022), *Inventory of Tax Technology Initiatives*, https://www.oecd.org/tax/forum-on-tax-administration/tax-technology-tools-and-digital-solutions/ (accessed on 13 May 2022). [1]

2 Responsibilities and collection

This chapter looks at the performance of tax administrations in discharging their primary role of collecting taxes. In this respect, it provides information on the aggregate net tax revenues collected as well as other key figures related to the activities of the administrations covered in this publication.

Introduction

The primary purpose of a tax administration is the collection of tax revenue to fund public services, but over time, many tax administrations have also been tasked with other responsibilities. This chapter provides an overview of the net tax revenues collected as well as some other key figures related to tax administration performance, and looks at the wider role tax administrations are playing in driving change across the whole of government.

Ongoing impact of the COVID-19 pandemic

Confidence in the proven ability of tax administrations to deliver complex administrative processes on a large scale was undoubtedly a key driver behind many governments giving their tax administrations additional responsibilities during the COVID-19 pandemic. While the 2021 version of the International Survey on Revenue Administration (ISORA) did not have detailed questions on additional responsibilities, interested readers may wish to consult Chapter 2 of *Tax Administration 2021* (OECD, 2021[1]) for a more detailed overview of the wider roles that tax administrations took on during the pandemic.

This highlighted that many of these new responsibilities often went beyond the functions normally provided by tax administrations and, typically, involved:

- **Financial assistance**, providing support to citizens and businesses, whether closely targeted or on a more universal basis;
- **Providing services**, using tax administration staff or services to support wider government COVID-19 responses; and
- **Information assistance**, supporting government by sharing information or using the administration's data analytics capabilities.

The reasons for turning towards tax administrations during the COVID-19 response included that tax administrations have:

- pre-existing close connections with citizens and businesses;
- long experience of operating at scale;
- skilled and specialised staff that interact with citizens on a daily basis;
- extensive data sets along with the analytical resources and experience in handling and sharing data.

Whilst many support measures remain in place, consideration is turning to the post pandemic environment. This is seeing many of the new ways of working undertaken in the rapid implementation of pandemic support schemes being integrated into business-as-usual practices. Tax administrations report that this has led to a number of longer-term shifts in the way they manage their business.

Box 2.1. Examples – COVID-19 changes

Indonesia – Managing service demand

The COVID-19 pandemic caused the Directorate General of Taxes (DGT) to innovate in their service provision, and this included the creation of an application to manage visits to tax office, named Kunjung Pajak. Services available through the app include an Integrated Service Counter, various consultations on tax matters as well as the Voluntary Disclosure Program.

Taxpayers access this service online and it allows DGT to manage the number of visitors according to the capacity of each unit, with quotas adjusted to meet the requirements of the pandemic. Tha app also

---

allows taxpayers to select the type of service and the time of arrival at the tax office. This not only helps improve tax services, but it also helps to prevent the spread of COVID-19. This is creating a digital archive of taxpayers who have interacted with DGT, including data on the type of service.

Romania - New electronic services offered to taxpayers

As part of their response to the pandemic, the National Agency for Fiscal Administration (NAFA) created a range of new electronic services to support taxpayers, and allow them to continue to interact with the tax administration. These included the creation of electronic filing of double taxation relief forms, video identification so that taxpayers could access a virtual private space, Virtual Private Space applications, an online booking tool to manage the capacity of meetings with NAFA as well as an online chat service.

United States - Advancements to the Remote Work Environment

Due to COVID-19, an evaluation of key examination activities that could not be conducted in a remote environment was made. As a result, Large Business and International (LB&I) implemented three key solutions: service wide guidance that allows for acceptance of a broad range of digital signatures; allowing password encrypted attachments to be transmitted to/from taxpayers; and a virtual closure process that allowed LB&I examiners/case processors to transmit case closing documents via email.

LB&I continues to collaborate across the organisation including with the Small Business/Self Employed Division on Centralized Case Processing to implement the mandatory 100% paperless case file closing process. There is also currently a pilot program for implementation of paperless case closings of returns with unique situations. Other initiatives such as various allowable digital signatures and encrypted password protections in transmission to/from taxpayers are expected to continue.

While the goal of these initiatives was to continue service during the pandemic, these improvements are expected to continue to improve the efficiency for taxpayers.

Sources: Indonesia (2022), Romania (2022) and the United States (2022).

The impact of COVID-19 on net revenue collections

As noted earlier, the information from the survey analysed for this chapter is showing the first impacts of the COVID-19 pandemic on revenue collection, which has seen revenue collections decreasing in more than three-quarters of administrations (see Table 2.1). Reasons for these falls include:

- **Decrease in economic activity**: COVID-19 related lockdown measures were introduced by many governments. The forced closure of many businesses will have negatively affected the taxable income and sales of many businesses and may have led to a temporary increase in business insolvencies and bankruptcies.
- **Increases in unemployment**: the decrease in economic activity may also have impacted on employment levels as businesses lay-off staff or pause recruitment.
- **Policy support measures**: To support consumption and the health system, many jurisdictions introduced temporary reductions in standard and reduced VAT rates. (OECD, 2020[2])
- **Administrative support measures**: Many tax administrations have taken measures to ease the burdens on taxpayers and to support businesses and individuals with cash flow problems or with difficulties in meeting tax payment obligations. Measures introduced include the extension of payment deadlines, deferral of tax payments and easier access to debt payment plans as well as the extension of plan duration.[1] While in many cases this may lead to timing differences in the receipt of tax payments due, in some cases the additional debt built up may become unrecoverable.

Table 2.1. Change in total net revenue collections between 2018 and 2019 as well as 2019 and 2020

Percent of administrations

Change in total net revenue collections	Between 2018 and 2019	Between 2019 and 2020
Increase	98	21
Decrease	2	79

Source: Table A.2 Net revenue collected by the tax administration: Total.

Responsibilities of tax administrations

With few exceptions, jurisdictions have unified the collection of direct and (most) indirect taxes within a single body for tax administration. (See Table 2.2 for the revenue types for which the tax administrations participating in this publication have responsibility.)

Table 2.2. Revenue types for which the tax administration has responsibility, 2020

Percent of administrations that have responsibility for the following revenue types

Personal income tax	Corporate income tax	Value added tax	Excises - domestic	Motor vehicle taxes	Real property taxes	Wealth taxes	Estate, inheritance, gift and other taxes	Other taxes on good and services	Social security contributions	Customs
98	100	93	60	48	45	22	52	50	40	45

Source: Table A.1 Revenue types for which the administration has responsibility and employer withholding.

However, as found in previous editions of the Tax Administration Series, governments have given tax administrations other areas of responsibility (including shared responsibility in some areas) in addition to their traditional tax roles.

Typically these may be to provide financial benefits to taxpayers (for example, welfare-type benefits) or to collect loans or debts owing to government (for example, student loans or child support). In other situations, the role/function is less directly related to the tax system, for example oversight of certain gambling activities or population registries. Some tax administrations report that following their successful implementation of COVID-19 support schemes, additional responsibilities are being given to them on a more permanent basis.

Box 2.2. Examples - New responsibilities

Australia - Introduction of Director ID register

The Australian Taxation Office (ATO) is the lead agency for the Modernising Business Registers (MBR) program in Australia. The MBR program aims to streamline how businesses register, view, and maintain their business information with government by bringing together multiple aged business registers onto a modern registry platform. This will make it easier for businesses to meet their registration obligations, make business information more trusted and valuable, and improve the efficiency of registry service interactions.

The first milestone in the program was the recent introduction of a director identification number (director ID) – a unique identifier that a director will apply for once and keep forever. An individual must confirm their identity to be able to receive a director ID. Director ID assists in identifying and eliminating director involvement in unlawful activity, such as illegal 'phoenixing' which is estimated to cost the Australian community between AUD 2.9 billion and AUD 5.1 billion every year. Director ID also helps prevent the use of false and fraudulent director identities and make it easier for government regulators to trace directors' relationships with companies over time.

United States - Child Tax Credit Update Portal

The American Rescue Plan of 2021 temporarily expanded eligibility for the Child Tax Credit (CTC) benefit and provided advance monthly payments of the tax credit to be sent to all eligible families. The Internal Revenue Service (IRS) was tasked with not only distributing over USD 94 billion of Advance CTC payments during 2021, but also providing new digital tools to assist taxpayers in managing their payments.

IRS launched the CTC Update Portal in June 2021. This initial launch was completed in 98 days and allowed families to check eligibility for advance payments, view monthly payment amounts, and un-enrol from advance payments to receive a lump sum in their 2021 tax refund. Over the following six months, the IRS developed this further and included major firsts for IRS digital capabilities such as functions to: update bank account, update mailing address, update household income as well as Spanish language browsing.

During 2021, the CTC Update Portal served 7 million unique users across 40 million total site visits. By providing these services online, IRS was able to not only provide improved customer service, but also create internal operational efficiencies.

Sources: Australia (2022) and the United States (2022).

Revenue collections

This section looks at the net revenue collection of tax administrations as well as a number of other key figures related to their activities.

Net collections by tax administrations averages 21% of jurisdiction GDP

Through its Global Revenue Statistics Database (OECD, 2022[3]) the OECD generally seeks to publish internationally comparable data on the tax revenues of its members as well as a number of other jurisdictions for all levels of government. As the information contained in the Global Revenue Statistics

Database reports data at a jurisdiction and not an administration level, tax administrations were asked in the ISORA survey to provide a range of information on their revenue collection activity. This information aptly demonstrates the importance of tax administrations to the respective economies.

Net revenue collected by tax administrations participating in this report, as a percentage of gross domestic product (GDP) in 2020 ranges from less than 10% to reach more than 30% in the case of Croatia, Norway, the Netherlands, Hungary, Latvia, Slovenia, Estonia, Denmark and Sweden. Average net revenue collected by administrations in this report is 21% of GDP (see Figure 2.1).

Net collections by tax administrations averages 61% total jurisdiction revenue

Forty-one tax administrations report net revenue collections exceeding more than 50% of total government revenue in 2020, making tax administrations the principle government revenue collection agency in more than two-thirds of jurisdictions covered in this report. Average net revenue collected by administrations in this report is 61% of total jurisdiction revenue (see Figure 2.2).

Figure 2.1. Net revenue collected as a percent of gross domestic product, 2020

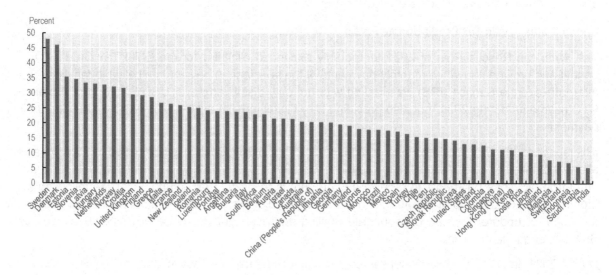

Source: Table D.1. Revenue related ratios

StatLink ᘒ᠌ᶠᶦᶫ https://doi.org/10.1787/888934310423

Figure 2.2. Net revenue collected as a percent of total government revenue, 2020

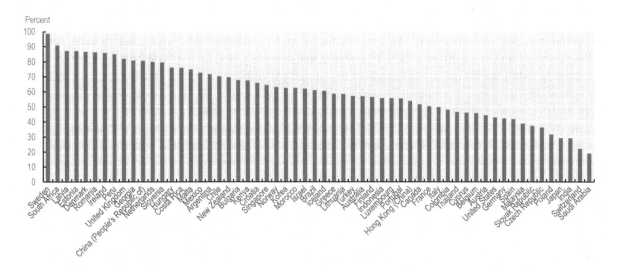

Source: Table D.1 Revenue related ratios

StatLink 🔗 https://doi.org/10.1787/888934310442

Value added tax and personal income tax account for 29% and 27% of net revenue collections, respectively, and are the major tax types collected by around 40% of the tax administrations covered in this report. Corporate Income Tax (17%) and social security contributions (10%) comprise the other major revenue types as reflected in Figure 2.3 In many jurisdictions, social security contributions are not collected by tax administrations and are therefore underrepresented when looking at average net revenue collections for all jurisdictions covered in this publication. Where collected, they are often the predominant source of tax revenue (see Table D.2).

Figure 2.3. Average net revenue collections (in percent) by major revenue type, 2020

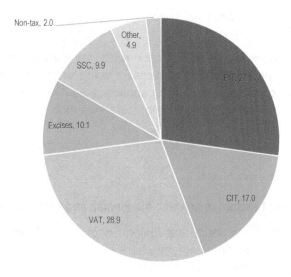

Source: Tables D.1 Revenue related ratios and D.2 Tax structure and SSC proportions.

StatLink 🔗 https://doi.org/10.1787/888934310461

Streamlining collections: Withholding at source

Withholding regimes can form part of compliance-by-design approaches which support overall compliance while significantly reducing burdens for large numbers of taxpayers depending on the extent of taxpayer involvement in any post-payment adjustments that might be needed (i.e. where withholding results in under-payment or over-payment of tax). In place of self-reporting and paying, withholding taxes are taxes paid directly to the tax administration, usually by a principal who pays the net income to the recipient (for example withholding by an employer on salary paid to an employee), or by an intermediary between the payer and customer. The most common withholding tax in operation globally is income tax on employment income (so called Pay-As-You-Earn (PAYE) approaches). Other examples include withholding taxes on interest, dividends or royalties. Depending on the underlying tax regime and nature of the payments, withholding can vary from a simple system, at a universal set rate, to a more complex system that is responsive to the customer's wider circumstances.[2]

In addition to minimising burdens, withholding regimes can also reduce misreporting and underpayment as principals or intermediaries responsible for forwarding taxes to the administration have no right over the respective amounts. Of course, there remains scope for failures in such approaches by misapplication of rules or errors by principals or intermediaries where the system relies on them providing information. However, increased automation, greater cross-checking of data and whole of government approaches have the potential to reduce such issues.

To understand the importance of withholding at source for personal income taxes, the survey underlying this publication asked participating administrations to estimate the percentage of total personal income tax withheld by third parties and subsequently paid to the administration. Administrations that were able to provide this information estimate that around 80% of total personal income tax collections were withheld at source in 2020 (see Table 2.3).

Table 2.3. Average percentage of personal income tax withholding between 2018 to 2020

2018	2019	2020	Difference in percentage points between 2018 and 2020
78.9	78.6	80.2	+1.3

Note: The table shows the average percentage of personal income tax withholding for 42 jurisdictions that were able to provide the information for the years 2018 to 2020.
Source: Table D.18 Electronic payment proportions and third party withholding.

Given the importance of these taxes to overall collection rates, tax administrations are investing in new and innovative approaches that can both reduce burdens for taxpayers such as prefilling tax returns with existing data from a wide range of sources, and using sophisticated analytics to identify non-compliance risks. This is a frequent theme throughout this edition of the series, and is covered in more detail in later chapters.

Box 2.3. Examples - Innovations in collection

Finland - Real-time tax information exchange between the Finnish and Estonian Tax Administrations

The economic relationship between Estonia and Finland is close, and has a direct impact on the respective tax administrations. In an environment where companies, individuals and money move quickly, swift access to information has become crucial. Real-time exchange of information supports both control actions and real-time audits and is especially important for detecting tax frauds. It can also improve the quality of taxpayers services.

To meet the need for real-time information, the tax administrations in both countries have implemented a unique information exchange structure that provides real-time access to predefined information held in the tax databases of the other administration. The exchanges operate through an API request and response messages are sent via interconnected secure national data exchange layer services.

The project planning started in 2020. First deployments were in 2021 when the Estonian Tax and Customs Board developed two services, VAT information and salary payments, for the use of the Finnish Tax Administration. In addition, the already existing Estonian service on tax debts was also included. The Finnish Tax Administration developed two services for the Estonian Tax and Customs Board, which were salaries received and salaries paid. More services will be developed in 2022.

Exchanges are considered as requests for information. The legal base for the exchanges is the Convention on Mutual Administrative Assistance in Tax Matters, supplemented by a bilateral Competent Authority Agreement.

See Annex 2.A for supporting material.

New Zealand - Automatic tax assessments

Planning for the 2021 automatic assessment season continued to build on lessons learnt from 2020 and 2019. New Zealand worked to get the assessments out faster to give customers certainty faster, and used the data throughout the year to help ensure people are paying and receiving the right amounts.

If deductions are accurate throughout the year, customers should have smaller refunds or bills to pay (if any) at the end of the tax year. New Zealand proactively contacted 450 000 customers and employers throughout the year to let them know that they were on unsuitable tax codes and needed to update their details.

As changes to employment and investment income reporting were introduced progressively, the year ending 31 March 2021 was the first full year New Zealand received more details, more often, about recipients of investment income. Income from portfolio investment entities—such as KiwiSaver schemes—is included in the end-of-year income tax assessment process and automated where possible.

New Zealand issued over 3.2 million assessments to customers through the 2021 process, with a 10% increase in tax assessments finalised, from 2.79 million assessments finalised in 2020 to 3.05 million in 2021.

There has also been year-on-year improvement in the accuracy of income tax assessments resulting in refunds. The average debit value decreased from NZD 559 in 2020 to NZD 454 in 2021.

See Annex 2.A for supporting material.

Sources: Finland (2022) and New Zealand (2022).

Note

[1] For a detailed description of support measures taken by tax administration, please see the 2020 note *Tax administration responses to COVID-19: Measures taken to support taxpayers* (CIAT/IOTA/OECD, 2020[5]).

[2] For further information on the withholding regimes put in place in jurisdictions, please see *Tax Administration 2019* (OECD, 2019[4]), Tables A.73 and A.74.

References

CIAT/IOTA/OECD (2020), "Tax administration responses to COVID-19: Measures taken to support taxpayers", *OECD Policy Responses to Coronavirus (COVID-19)*, OECD Publishing, Paris, https://doi.org/10.1787/adc84188-en. [5]

OECD (2022), *Global Revenue Statistics Database*, https://www.oecd.org/tax/tax-policy/global-revenue-statistics-database.htm (accessed on 13 May 2022). [3]

OECD (2021), *Tax Administration 2021: Comparative Information on OECD and other Advanced and Emerging Economies*, OECD Publishing, Paris, https://doi.org/10.1787/cef472b9-en. [1]

OECD (2020), *Tax policy responses to COVID-19; table with measures takes by countries*, http://www.oecd.org/tax/covid-19-tax-policy-and-other-measures.xlsm (accessed on 13 May 2022). [2]

OECD (2019), *Tax Administration 2019: Comparative Information on OECD and other Advanced and Emerging Economies*, OECD Publishing, Paris, https://doi.org/10.1787/74d162b6-en. [4]

Annex 2.A. Links to supporting material (accessed on 13 May 2022)

- Box 2.3. – Finland: Link to a presentation with more details on the real-time exchanges with Estonia: https://www.oecd.org/tax/forum-on-tax-administration/database/b.2.3-finland-real-time-exchanges-with-estonia.pdf
- Box 2.3. – New Zealand: Link to a case study looking at the outcomes of automatically issuing income tax assessments after the third year of operation: https://www.oecd.org/tax/forum-on-tax-administration/database/b.2.3-tas2022-new-zealand-year-three-of-automatically-issued-income-tax-assessments.pdf

3 Registration and identification

A comprehensive system of taxpayer registration and identification is critical for the effective operation of a tax system. This chapter comments on some of the issues that are of significance for registration and identification processes.

Introduction

A comprehensive system of taxpayer registration and identification is critical for the effective operation of a tax system. It is the basis for supporting self-assessment, value-added tax and withholding tax regimes, as well as third party reporting and matching. This chapter comments on five issues of significance in taxpayer registration and identification: levels of registration, registration channels, integration with other parts of government, identity management, and emerging common approaches to digital identity.

Levels of registration

The fundamental importance of an effective tax registration system cannot be underestimated. Tax administrations need strong processes to both manage those taxpayers that are "part of the system" and to help them identify those yet to register. Furthermore, they need to be able to monitor and determine actions and interventions to establish any liability to tax for both individuals and corporate bodies, even in systems where filing is not mandatory.

Figure 3.1 provides information on the rate of registered personal taxpayers as a percentage of the total population. This shows a wide range of registration rates, often reflecting the level of integration the tax administration has with other parts of government.

Figure 3.1. Registration of active personal income taxpayers as percentage of population, 2020

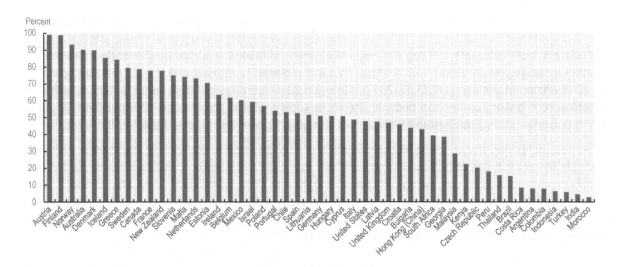

Source: Table D.10 Registration of personal income taxpayers.

StatLink https://doi.org/10.1787/888934310480

Registration channels

While the majority of administrations are solely responsible for the system of registration for tax purposes within their jurisdictions, previous editions of this series have shown that in many jurisdictions the registration processes can also be initiated outside of the tax administration through other government agencies (OECD, 2019[1]).

Figure 3.2. Availability of registration channels for taxpayers, 2020

Percent of administrations that provide the respective registration channel

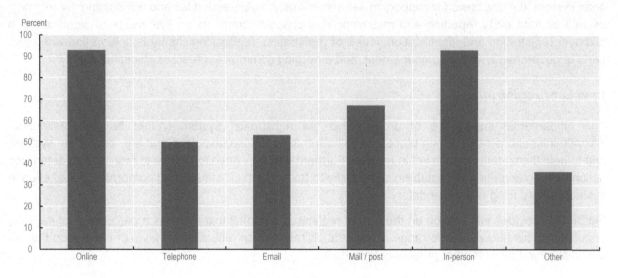

Note: The registration channels may not always be available for all tax types or taxpayer segments.
Source: Table A.39 Registration channels.

StatLink ᴍᴀᴛ ꕷ https://doi.org/10.1787/888934310499

In looking at how taxpayers can register, almost all administrations reported they provide more than one channel for taxpayers to use and 93% report that it is possible to register online. Compared to data from the 2017 edition of this series (OECD, 2017[2]) this is a 23 percentage point increase. In fact, together with in-person registration, online has become the most widely offered registration channel (see Figure 3.2) and in one jurisdiction (Saudi Arabia), taxpayers can only register online (see Table A.39).

While the underlying survey does not allow identification of whether the online registration channel is available for all tax types or taxpayer segments, tax administrations report significant investment in digital identity programmes, including using artificial intelligence to improve efficiency and effectiveness. This is helping cement digital identity as the cornerstone of successful digitalisation activity. The shift to digital channels may also help drive further efficiencies. Figure 3.2 highlights the continuing high level of in-person offerings, which is often an expensive service channel.

Box 3.1. Examples – registration channels

Canada - Use of provincial digital identities

The Canada Revenue Agency (CRA) is continually looking to improve service delivery and regularly receives feedback on its services. The Agency has heard from its clients that it can be challenging to remember multiple usernames and passwords, especially as organizations require users to create more complex passwords.

In support of the Pan-Canadian Trust Framework, the CRA, as part of the federal government, sought provincial partnerships to be able to leverage their provincial digital IDs. This allows citizens to use their provincial credentials to access CRA services instead of having to create another username/password.

As provinces are the issuers of foundational documents (e.g. birth certificates, health cards, driver's licenses, etc.) with in-person services, they are well placed to identity proof individuals.

The CRA is currently partnered with the province of British Columbia (BC). From February 2020 to December 2021: 223 107 individuals (unique users) have used their BC Services Card credentials to sign-in to CRA's secure portals, representing close to 2 million sign-ins (1 976 674). As additional provinces establish digital identity programs, the CRA will explore future partnerships.

China (People's Republic of) - Digital identity supporting smart taxation

The State Taxation Administration (STA) is building a national network to provide a secure and consistent digital identity, laying a solid foundation for smart taxation. Based on legal identity and a national authoritative authentication source, the digital identity connects legal persons and natural persons handling tax related business on behalf of enterprises. This is done through confirmation by both parties, and covers all taxpayers, and supports accurate services and management of taxpayers.

Over 80% of taxpayers use an approved digital identity to access secure digital services offered by STA including comprehensive information reporting, tax declaration and payment, certificate issuance, tax refunds, tax administrative licenses and other tax issues. Taxpayers are also allowed to authorise third parties to represent businesses and access secure digital services.

With the digital identity, the scope to save costs is increased as taxpayers only need to register in one place. This can then be recognised in other places, and the digital identity can also connect identities via across devices, and applications. It also provides the ability to allow taxpayers to choose a variety of authentication and login approaches, such as Short Message Service (SMS), ID card, digital certificate, and face recognition.

With the continuous development of the national network of digital identity, it will further provide unified and authoritative identity services for all taxpayers and tax officials to facilitate smooth progress of the digital transformation of the People's Republic of China's tax collection and administration.

Georgia - Taxation of Digital Services

From 2021 taxable persons, who are not established, have no habitual residence, or have no permanent establishment in Georgia are obliged to register and pay VAT if they are engaged in the supply of digital services. Digital services include telecommunication, radio or television broadcasting and electronically supplied services.

To support this, the Georgia Revenue Service (GRS) designed a special platform, VAT Portal on Digital Services, for a simplified registration and reporting process. While developing this new measure, GRS studied international practice in the taxation of digital services and consulted with Business at OECD (BIAC). The VAT portal is therefore a product of intensive communication with stakeholders who contributed their experiences and views in developing simplified registration and reporting systems for VAT payers. Tax can also be paid in both Georgian Lari and foreign currencies (USD or EUR) which can be selected at the time of the registration on the VAT portal.

Sweden – Artificial Intelligence (AI) in business registration

The Swedish Tax Agency's risk-evaluation service for business registration applications was launched in May 2021. This AI-based service categorises applications based on a set of established risk factors, and applications are then processed in different ways, depending on the category assigned.

The Swedish Tax Agency receives about 300 000 applications per year. About 70% of applications to register a business in Sweden are completed digitally, and approximately 95% of these digital applications are entirely automated.

Previously, the categorisation process was manual and very time consuming. After less than one year in operation, the first version of the risk-evaluation service has already yielded a solid return on investment with business registration process shortened by up to six days and a cost reduction of SEK 28 million (approximately 16% of the total cost of the business registration process).

Further developments took place during 2021, including the introduction of risk-evaluation support for paper-based applications for business registration. In early 2022, robotic process automation (RPA) was introduced for low-risk applications. So far, about 450 applications per week – a total of 1 300 – have been processed using RPA, further contributing to the benefits.

Sources: Canada (2022), China (People's Republic of) (2022), Georgia (2022) and Sweden (2022).

Integration with other parts of government

Given the pivotal role that registration and taxpayer identification play in underpinning the tax system, having up-to-date tax registers will is a high priority for most tax administrations. As past editions have shown, the large majority of administrations have formal programmes in place to improve the quality of the tax register (OECD, 2019[1]).

Therefore, it is unsurprising that other government bodies may wish to use the tax administration register for their own purposes to provide services to citizens or ensure compliance with laws and regulations. This is leading to the creation of cross government databases. As Figure 3.3 illustrates, 70% of administrations report the existence of a range of available databases.

Increased integration across government became even more relevant during the COVID-19 pandemic, when a number of governments saw the potential in using information maintained by tax administrations, such as taxpayer address and bank information, to contact citizens and businesses or to make direct benefit or support payments (OECD, 2020[3]).

The pandemic has also highlighted the need for closer collaboration with other government agencies, and many administrations are integrating their IT systems to make tax registration part of other actions taxpayers undertake. For example registering for tax at the same time as registering a company or registering the birth of a child; and/or to use the same identifier to allow taxpayers to access other government services.

Figure 3.3. Cross government databases: Availability and database types, 2022

Percent of jurisdictions

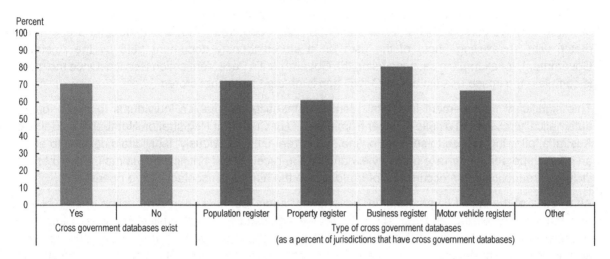

Note: The figure is based on ITTI data from 52 jurisdictions that are covered in this report and that have completed the global survey on digitalisation.
Source: OECD et al (2022), Inventory of Tax Technology Initiatives, https://www.oecd.org/tax/forum-on-tax-administration/tax-technology-tools-and-digital-solutions/, Table DM3 (accessed on 13 May 2022).

StatLink https://doi.org/10.1787/888934310518

In this context, many governments are now using, implementing or considering a unique and secure identification system for citizens and businesses to allow for a greater joining-up of systems and services.

Box 3.2. Examples - Collaboration on digital identity

Argentina – Single tax registry

The development and implementation of the RUT system (Single Tax Registry), is a result of the collaboration between the Federal Administration of Public Revenue and the provincial collection agencies to improve, simplify and modernize the actions that taxpayers have to take to fulfill their tax obligations. In addition, it guarantees a higher quality of information for all Argentine tax administrations.

Previously, taxpayers had to register and maintain data in several different registries. The loading of the same data in completely different registries resulted in a loss of time for the taxpayer, and multiple errors and inconsistencies across the databases. This meant it was very difficult to conduct cross-validations between agencies.

Now, through a block chain, the data from the Federal Registry is shared in almost real-time with the participating agencies. The benefits of this federal tool are that the taxpayer does not have to upload the data to several tax administrations, leading to higher quality data which adheres to the principle of uniqueness of the data. This is also leading to a reduction in the administrative management time in the event of errors and/or inconsistencies.

See Annex 3.A for supporting material.

Australia – Whole of Government ID Programme

The Australian Government's Digital Identity Program aims to make it easier for Australians to securely access Government online services. The Australian Tax Office (ATO) was responsible for delivering myGovID and part this was the ability to determine that a photo taken by a user of the myGovID app is of a true and live person. With user consent, the image captured is used to undertake a one-to-one match with an existing photo of the user on a stored identity document held by the Australian Government, for example a passport using the Government's Face Verification Service. Once the match is complete the image used in the myGovID app is deleted and is not stored.

This significant improvement in Digital Identity authentication enables individuals to apply for and automatically receive a Tax File Number from the ATO or Customer Registration Number from Services Australia, allowing access to services online and in real-time. Previously, individuals needed to attend an office in person, undertake an interview and wait to receive their notification via mail. Other benefits include a reduction in the occurrence of fraud and to the burden on contact centre operations.

As a result of the digital ID programme, government agencies have seen a reduction in call volumes and manual processing and the ability to re-use functionality to streamline services. Benefits to taxpayers have been significant during the COVID-19 pandemic as they have been able to easily access government stimulus support measures, anywhere, anytime, without the need to attend an office or endure delays due to processing times.

Italy - Whole of government digital identity

In 2016, the Italian Revenue Agency has introduced the possibility for taxpayers to access the pre-filled income tax return using the Public Digital Identity System (SPID). In 2018, access via SPID was extended to all services provided in the "reserved area" of the Revenue Agency. From 2021, in addition to SPID, taxpayers may also use Electronic Identity Card (CIE). This means that, all citizens, including those authorized to operate on behalf of legal persons, can now access the "reserved area" through SPID and CIE credentials.

This means for example that SPID allows the registration of leasing contracts, the consultation of electronic invoices, the submission of pre-filled income tax returns, as well as the submission of documentation necessary to solve irregularities notified to taxpayers.

See Annex 3.A for supporting material.

Netherlands - Exploring Self Sovereign Identity (SSI)

The Dutch Government's Digital Identity Program is exploring solutions for giving citizens and businesses highly secure digital identities as well as more control over their (personal) data. As a contributor to this program, the Netherlands Tax Administration (NTA) found two main concepts for SSI based solutions:

- The first concept is based upon a Digital Identity Wallet that supports functions that include: secure access, digital signing and mandate services, and real-time data management. The first working prototype provided a validated statement of income to a citizen that can be shared at their own discretion with several (private) service providers. The conclusion was SSI can support easier tax services, enhance privacy and transparency and reduce the need for reporting and auditing.

- The second concept is a Legal Entity Wallet; the NTA participated in a proof-of-concept exercise 'Digitally starting an Enterprise'. The concept has been worked out through every step from the civil-law notary to establishing the wallet, registration at the Chamber of Commerce, the NTA issuing the VAT number ID and the opening of a bank account. The 'enterprise wallet' provides more certainty in the proceedings and is used to collect and share verifiable credentials. NTA expects more tax related services can be added to this wallet, creating a brand new channel of interaction.

Sources: Argentina (2022), Australia (2022), Italy (2022) and the Netherlands (2022).

Identity management

All tax administrations, whether required to by law or as a matter of sound business practice, put considerable effort into ensuring the security of taxpayer information. In addition to internal processes to prevent unlawful attempts to obtain information and to ensure taxpayers' rights are protected, all administrations have processes to ensure the person they are dealing with is in fact the taxpayer. Increasingly these approaches, which in many instances have now been extended to multi-step authentication, are making use of biometric information, unique to the taxpayer.

Tax administrations face similar challenges to other organisations in dealing with individuals or organisations that may misuse personal information to impersonate taxpayers in order to commit fraud. The on-going and, in many cases, organised nature of this activity is requiring administrations to devote considerable effort to the prevention of identity theft through staff training and increased security. Box 3.3 contains examples of the work tax administrations are doing in this respect.

Box 3.3. Examples – Identity management

Canada - Multi-factor Authentication

In response to increasing cyber-attacks, the CRA enhanced its security with the introduction of multi-factor authentication (MFA) to the 14.6 million online account holders. Initially, MFA was implemented only allowing for one-time passcodes to be issued by SMS or through a voice message to those with a North American phone number.

Once implemented, it became clear that this MFA solution did not fit all users. CRA received feedback from segments of the taxpayer population, such as those without a phone, those with only international phone numbers and business communities. The CRA held further dialogue with its stakeholders to understand their challenges and barriers.

As a result of these discussions, the CRA developed a supplementary non-phone method of MFA, the passcode grid (PCG). The PCG is a printable, randomly generated grid of characters, similar to a bingo card. For those that choose this method, users are prompted for the characters from various coordinates on this grid at each login.

With the implementation of this enhancement, the CRA is able to retain a strong security position but also respond to user needs such that all Canadians are well served. With the addition of the PCG, the CRA was able to achieve its security goals and adopt mandatory MFA for 100% of its users.

Finland - Security awareness

E-mail phishing has been recognised as a constantly evolving security threat in the Finnish Tax Administration (Vero). Since phishing can potentially affect all staff, Vero has started to use automated, gamified phishing simulations to make staff more resistant to phishing attacks.

The awareness program teaches users to identify and report malicious e-mails. The training does not require much time. On average, users receive a simulation e-mail every other week, taking 3-5 minutes of their time. Simulations are sent directly to users' inboxes, users report them and receive a micro training in the portal if they wish. As staff members can never know which emails are part of the training and which are genuine, the simulations make security awareness a part of everyone's daily work life thus keeping them alert at all times.

In practice, users are asked to report all suspicious e-mails via a simple reporting button, available upon installing in their Outlook programme. The threshold for reporting is very low, and the game develops with the users: the more e-mails you report, the harder they become for you to identify. Using the same reporting button for all suspicious e-mails helps Vero catch genuine phishing as well as train the staff.

The automated gamified phishing simulation tool has proven to be very effective, with Vero successfully catching real threats due to early reporting. Furthermore, as the tool takes care of the content of the simulation messages, so Vero does not have to use much time or other resources to create new material.

United States - Secure Access Digital Identity (SADI)

In 2021, the Internal Revenue Service (IRS) accelerated the development and launch of Secure Access Digital Identity (SADI) as a new online identity verification platform for accessing self-help tools on the IRS.gov website. SADI was designed and implemented as the next generation identity proofing solution to improve taxpayer access to IRS online services while also meeting digital identity guidelines established by the National Institute of Standards and Technology.

This new process is revolutionising how the IRS identity proofs and authenticates taxpayers by implementing a federated approach to authentication that includes working with a third-party Credential Service Provider (CSP). CSPs are trusted technology providers that conduct identity proofing and credential management services for access to digital services, now including IRS online tools. This federated approach allows taxpayers to access applications across different, participating agencies using a single set of credentials trusted by multiple parties. It also extends access to more users by offering an expanded set of documents to verify identities, as well as offering improved help desk services and support for multiple languages.

The IRS is in the process of migrating all online protected applications behind the modernised SADI platform. From 21 June 2021 through 31 December 2021, 5.9 million taxpayers successfully created their SADI credentials, which accounted for 23.1 million online sessions, making this IRS program the largest digital identity federation in US history.

Sources: Canada (2022), Finland (2022) and the United States (2022).

Common approaches to Digital identity

Once the domain of multi-national businesses and those involved in international trade, small and medium-sized enterprises and individual taxpayers are now increasingly earning income sourced outside their jurisdiction of residence. As a result of the proliferation of online market places and sharing and gig economy platforms, it is now easier than ever for example, to rent out holiday homes or sell goods abroad through online platforms.

Tax administrations are facing a raft of issues in supporting and responding to this growth in cross-border activity, including how they manage taxpayer information flows across borders. Previous editions of the tax administration series (OECD, 2019[1]) highlighted two international measures aimed at helping administrations to address these issues:

- The European Union's Electronic Identification Authentication and Trust Services (eIDAS) approach, which was introduced in 2014 and aims at increasing the confidence taxpayers and tax administrations can have in dealing with information flows and being able to manage identity and registration issues across borders.
- The global standard on Automatic Exchange of Information (AEOI) – the Common Reporting Standard (CRS), which together with the United States Foreign Account Tax Compliance Act (FATCA) provides for the exchange of non-resident financial account information with the tax authorities in the account holders' jurisdiction of tax residence.

Following the 2019 OECD report *The Sharing and Gig Economy: Effective Taxation of Platform Sellers* (OECD, 2019[4]), the OECD published in 2020 a set of Model Rules that set the framework for digital platforms to collect information on the income realised by those offering accommodation, transport and personal services through platforms and to report the information to tax authorities. A key objective for the Model Rules is to help taxpayers be compliant with their tax obligations, and to provide a consistent framework to help business provide information to tax authorities. This supports the Model Rules goal of streamlining reporting regimes for tax administrations and platform operators alike. (OECD, 2020[5])

Around the same time, the OECD *Tax Administration 3.0* report (OECD, 2020[6]) identified the seamless taxation of platform sellers as a key action for multilateral collaboration. Work is currently ongoing to explore how co-operation between administrations and platforms can be deepened to explore the integration of identification and reporting processes into the applications used by the platforms in order to support tax compliance by platform sellers as well as reducing burdens for all parties.

More generally, common approaches to digital identity that are shared across government, and between government and third parties, will increasingly allow new services to be developed. These services can reduce burdens on taxpayers as third parties can supply information direct to tax administrations, as well as providing richer and more accurate pools of data to tax administrations.

Box 3.4. Canada - Third party authorisations

To help taxpayers protect their personal and tax information, the CRA recently introduced a new digital two-step verification process to confirm the authorization of third-party representatives in its digital portals. This change made it easier for individuals and businesses to confirm who can access their personal and tax information and help them play an active role in protecting this information. Whether the taxpayer is an individual or a business, they can now confirm third party requests for access to their personal and tax information by signing in to the secure portals, without waiting for a confirmation call from the CRA.

For all but a few exceptions, this innovative process saved the CRA from having to contact individuals and businesses by telephone to verify requests for authorizations received, saving time and resources on the part of both the CRA and its clients. With this new process, individuals and business owners can confirm the requests on their own time and representatives are able to track the status of their requests online.

Before the process was implemented, additional staff needed to be hired and trained to handle the number of confirmation calls that needed to be made. Since its implementation, the amount of confirmation calls required have decreased by 88% (or 5 278 total calls made since implementation versus 42 314 calls over the same period last year).

Source: Canada (2022).

References

OECD (2020), *Model Rules for Reporting by Platform Operators with respect to Sellers in the Sharing and Gig Economy*, OECD, Paris, http://www.oecd.org/tax/exchange-of-tax-information/model-rules-for-reporting-by-platform-operators-with-respect-to-sellers-in-the-sharing-and-gig-economy.htm (accessed on 13 May 2022). [5]

OECD (2020), *Tax Administration 3.0: The Digital Transformation of Tax Administration*, OECD, Paris, https://www.oecd.org/tax/forum-on-tax-administration/publications-and-products/tax-administration-3-0-the-digital-transformation-of-tax-administration.htm (accessed on 13 May 2022). [6]

OECD (2020), "Tax administration responses to COVID-19: Assisting wider government", *OECD Policy Responses to Coronavirus (COVID-19)*, OECD Publishing, Paris, https://doi.org/10.1787/0dc51664-en. [3]

OECD (2019), *Tax Administration 2019: Comparative Information on OECD and other Advanced and Emerging Economies*, OECD Publishing, Paris, https://doi.org/10.1787/74d162b6-en. [1]

OECD (2019), *The Sharing and Gig Economy: Effective Taxation of Platform Sellers : Forum on Tax Administration*, OECD Publishing, Paris, https://doi.org/10.1787/574b61f8-en. [4]

OECD (2017), *Tax Administration 2017: Comparative Information on OECD and Other Advanced and Emerging Economies*, OECD Publishing, Paris, https://doi.org/10.1787/tax_admin-2017-en. [2]

Annex 3.A. Links to supporting material (accessed on 13 May 2022)

- Box 3.2. – Argentina: Link to a flowchart that illustrates the process of updating registry data: https://www.oecd.org/tax/forum-on-tax-administration/database/b.3.2-argentina-rut.pdf
- Box 3.2. – Italy: Link to a website with information on how to access online services using the digital identity: https://www.agenziaentrate.gov.it/portale/web/english/how-to-access-the-online-services.

4 Assessment

This chapter looks at the tax assessment function, which includes all activities related to processing tax returns and payments. It comments on the use of e-channels for filing and paying, outlines administrations' efforts to provide pre-filled returns, and discusses the level of on-time return filing and payment. It also provides examples of the impact of technology and data sciences techniques on refund processes.

Introduction

The tax assessment function includes all activities related to processing tax returns, including issuing assessments, refunds, notices and statements. It also includes the processing and banking of payments. These activities continue to be an area of significant change and focus as administrations look to take costs out of high volume processes.

Previous editions of this series have highlighted how the widespread enabling of electronic filing and payment by taxpayers has helped administrations to reduce their costs and improve the services they provide. This trend has continued with an increasing range of supporting services and options now also being made available.

Tax administrations are also managing an expanding range of data that administrations are collecting electronically, including from a growing number of third party organisations. This is facilitating a shift towards more intelligent use of data, and more complete pre-filled returns, increasingly driven by the use of artificial intelligence and machine learning. This is also helping to create more upstream compliance approaches that can minimise or prevent errors in returns. As well as updating information on the use of channels used for filing and paying, this chapter will:

- Outline administrations' efforts to provide pre-filled returns for individual and corporate taxpayers, including the expansion of this approach by some into "no-return regimes";
- Discuss the levels of on-time return filing and payment; and
- Provide examples of how technology and the application of data sciences have improved refund processes.

Use of e-channels for filing and paying

With digitalisation continuing to transform everyday life, it is unsurprising that the uptake in the use of e-filing and payment channels continues to grow. Table 4.1 provides average e-filing rates from jurisdictions that provided details of channels used by taxpayers to file for the years 2018 to 2020. Over that period, more than nine-out-of-ten business taxpayers filed their returns electronically. For personal income tax return filers this figure is around 85%. Also, it should be noted that for a significant number of administrations a 100% e-filing rate has already become reality (see Table D.13 in the ISORA data).

Table 4.1. Average e-filing rates (in percent) by tax type

Tax type	2018	2019	2020
Personal income tax (47 jurisdictions)	80.0	82.4	85.6
Corporate income tax (50 jurisdictions)	92.3	93.4	94.2
Value added tax (44 jurisdictions)	96.2	96.9	97.8

Note: The table shows the average e-filing rates for those jurisdictions that were able to provide the information for the years 2018, 2019 and 2020. The number of jurisdictions for which data was available is shown in parenthesis
Source: Table D.13 Electronic filing.

Looking at the evolution of e-filing rates over the period 2014 to 2020 shown in Table 4.2, it is clear that e-filing rates have increased significantly – between 15 and 20 percentage points – across the three main tax types. (It should be noted that the table only takes into account information from jurisdictions for which data was available for both years 2014 and 2020, which explains the differences in 2020 averages shown in Tables 4.1 and 4.2)

Table 4.2. Evolution of e-filing rates (in percent) between 2014 and 2020 by tax type

Tax type	2014	2020	Difference in percentage points
Personal income tax (31 jurisdictions)	63.2	82.4	+19.2
Corporate income tax (33 jurisdictions)	76.3	94.9	+18.6
Value added tax (29 jurisdictions)	82.3	98.0	+15.7

Note: The table shows the average e-filing rates for those jurisdictions that were able to provide the information for the years 2014 and 2020. The number of jurisdictions for which data was available is shown in parenthesis
Source: Table D.13 Electronic filing and OECD (2017), *Tax Administration 2017: Comparative Information on OECD and Other Advanced and Emerging Economies*, Table A.8, https://doi.org/10.1787/tax_admin-2017-en.

As for electronic payments rates, as can be seen in Table 4.3, more than 85% of payments, measured by number and value, were made electronically in 2020. The percentage of e-payments by value is slightly higher than the percentage of e-payments made by number, suggesting that particularly larger taxpayers make use of this payment channel. (Due to a change in the definition of the underlying survey question, it is not possible to look at the evolution of e-payment rates since 2014.)

Table 4.3. Average e-payment rates (in percent) by number and value of payments

Measurement type	2018	2019	2020
Percentage by number of payments (47 jurisdictions)	79.9	82.1	86.3
Percentage by value of payments (47 jurisdictions)	84.4	85.8	88.4

Note: The table shows the average e-payment rates for those jurisdictions that were able to provide the information for the years 2018, 2019 and 2020. The number of jurisdictions for which data was available is shown in parenthesis.
Source: Table D.18 Electronic payment proportions and third party withholding.

There remain a number of jurisdictions where the volume of returns filed using paper as well as payments through non-electronic means remains high. Among those jurisdictions that provided data, more than 52 million returns (for PIT, CIT and VAT) were still filed on paper (see Tables A.45 to A.47). However, it should be acknowledged that this is a significant reduction compared to the years prior to the COVID-19 pandemic where, for the same set of jurisdictions, 88 million returns were filed on paper in 2018 and 75 million returns in 2019.

It is to be expected that this figure will further decline over time as more administrations take steps to encourage more taxpayers to use electronic platforms where possible. This will not only lower administration costs but could also reduce the administrative burden on taxpayers over time.

Box 4.1. Examples - E-filing

India - Integrated e-filing and centralised processing

The Integrated E-Filing and Centralized Processing Centre 2.0 (IEC 2.0) is a technology led innovation that aims to transform tax filing and processing. Beyond the core functions of e-Filing and processing of tax returns, this project has also helped taxpayer engagement and facilitation so that their issues can be resolved in more efficient and effective manner.

The project is achieving its objectives by making it easier to file returns using wizard-based forms, an intuitive user interface with simple questions to guide filing journey and generating pre-filled returns for the tax payers. More than 61 million returns were filed this way in fiscal year 2020-21. It is also actively promoting taxpayer education and e-verification of tax returns and has established a complete paperless environment. IEC 2.0 has reduced the processing time of returns on a year-on-year basis and is achieving real time processing of returns and credit of refunds.

IEC 2.0 has reduced errors, and is achieving its target of "first-time-right". Defective tax returns out of total tax returns filed have reduced from 1.05% for fiscal year 2019-20 to 0.0025% for fiscal year 2020-21. IEC 2.0 aims to provide convenience and simplicity through a "one-stop shop" for taxpayers, helping to reduce their compliance burden.

See Annex 4.A for supporting material.

Japan - Centralized corporation tax return filing

In Japan, large domestic enterprises, became required to submit electronically their tax return, including any attachments, for fiscal years beginning on or after 1 April 2020. With the introduction of this obligation, various measures have been taken to improve the convenience of taxpayers.

Until April 2020, these enterprises had needed to file their national and local tax returns through different electronic filing systems. Since then, thanks to the work to connect these systems, they have been able to remove duplicate inputs of common items in their national and local tax returns.

Secondly, until April 2020, enterprises had been required to submit their financial statements both to national and municipal governments when filing tax returns. To increase the convenience of taxpayers, they have now been able to remove the double submission of the financial statements with national and municipal governments sharing the information in the 'back office'.

Going forward, there will be more work to make electronic filing available to all corporations, not only large enterprises but also small and medium enterprises.

See Annex 4.A for supporting material.

Sources: India (2022) and Japan (2022).

Pre-filled returns

One of the significant innovations in tax return process design over the last two decades has been the development of pre-filled tax returns, often for personal income taxpayers. The pre-filled approach involves administrations "pre-populating" the taxpayer's return or on-line account with information from third parties. The pre-filled return can be reviewed by the taxpayer and either filed electronically or in paper form. As the extent of pre-population is generally determined by the range of electronic data sources available to the administration, it is critical to this approach that the legislative framework provides extensive and timely third party reporting covering as much relevant taxpayer information as possible.

The complexities of the legal frameworks governing tax can be a barrier to more automated tax calculations, and to help overcome this some tax administrations are exploring the use of machine readable legislation which can help automate the calculation process through the use of algorithms (see examples in Chapter 5). This is leading to reduced errors and reduced burdens for taxpayers.

Advocates of pre-filling initially encouraged its use with individual tax regimes that allowed relatively few deductions and credits, and where they could be verified with third party data sources. Advances in rules-based technologies, information-reporting requirements and the application of data science techniques mean that the approach can now be considered more widely. For example, survey responses show that in many jurisdictions PIT returns are now pre-filled with different income information as well as deductible expenses such as donations, school and university fees and insurance premiums (see Figures 4.1 and 4.2). The latest developments in some jurisdictions are described in Box 4.2.

In a growing number of jurisdictions, this concept now goes as far as totally pre-filling PIT returns, which the taxpayer then has to either agree (which may be by deemed agreement after a certain period of elapsed time) or provide further information which may lead to an upwards or downwards adjustment (see Table A.46). In their most advanced form, complete pre-filled returns are being generated for large proportions of the individual tax base. In addition, the availability of electronic invoicing systems allows tax administrations to start to go beyond PIT returns and pre-fill corporate income tax (CIT) and value-added tax (VAT) returns (see Tables A.45 and A.47).

Box 4.2. Examples - Pre-filling

Australia – Prefilling programme

Prefilling information is a very effective strategy for the Australian Taxation Office (ATO) in improving voluntary compliance and reducing the tax gap, which is currently at 5.6% for individual taxpayers. The ATO currently prefills approximately 90 million rows of data into the tax returns for individuals each year. This accounts for approximately 88% of all income amounts reported by individual taxpayers. Ninety percent of these are accepted without amendment by the taxpayer.

The Data Acquisition Prefilling and Sharing program is the next development in this work, and aims to deliver a modernised, end to end data ingestion and analytics solution that will address current limitations and enable more scalable and adaptable approaches to on-boarding datasets and enabling analytical outcomes.

Incrementally, existing workloads are being transitioned off legacy patterns onto the cloud-based solution and all new use cases will be built using the cloud-based solution. The capabilities of this solution will also be incrementally enhanced, driven by the specific needs of the use case but designed in a way to produce an inventory of re-usable building blocks that will enable quicker, lower cost delivery over time. The new platform will provide a number of significant benefits to the organisation, in particular it:

- Enables the decommissioning of legacy systems with rapidly diminishing workforce skills and knowledge
- Avoids significant costs associated with upgrading niche on-premise systems and their associated licence, support and maintenance costs
- Provides greater agility to respond to business demand and technology trends
- Enhances the ability to leverage new data sources more easily to sustainably reduce the tax gap, targeted at 4.5% for individuals.

Colombia – Prefilled tax returns

This project used the information reported by third parties to the Colombian Tax and Customs Administration (DIAN) to reduce compliance costs for individuals and legal entities. By using this information, DIAN can prefill some fields of the income tax return form that the taxpayer can then verify. This is part of DIAN's strategy of making it easier for taxpayers to file their tax returns.

The results of the project have been significant. For the taxable year 2019, the number of taxpayers to whom the pre-filled income tax return was issued increased 296.4%, going from 781 012 to 3 095 575 and for taxable year 2020 this trend continued, increasing to 4 102 239 taxpayers, which represents an increase of 32.5 % with respect the taxable year 2019.

The suggested income tax returns have brought not only benefits for the taxpayers but also for DIAN. For the 2019 tax year, a total of 268 861 individuals who previously had not filed income tax returns, did file returns and paid approximately COP 35 billion. For the 2020 tax year, the challenge was significant, taking into account the pandemic effects that decreased earnings of a significant number of people. Despite the impact of this situation, 576 416 people who had not been filling their income tax return, began to do so and made payments on an amount exceeding COP 111 billion.

Denmark - APIs (SOAP Web Services) to submit VAT returns

In Denmark, an API has been developed for operators of accounting software, which makes it possible for companies to transfer data directly from the accounting software to the VAT return system of the tax administration with only one approval required from the company.

The API consists of three main elements:

- The first web service returns dates by which the legal entity has to submit VAT Returns. These dates are required, when submitting VAT Returns.
- The second web service submits a draft of the VAT Returns to the tax administration at skat.dk with all the completed fields. The legal entity can access the submitted VAT Returns and approve it.
- The last web service provides a receipt for the VAT Returns given that the legal entity has approved it. This service also includes payment information on how to pay any outstanding balance.

The sample client for the service is free and can be used in all accounting software. The API has been operating since December 2019. So far eight suppliers have connected their accounting software to the solution, resulting in around 30 000 companies automatically submitting approximately 100 000 VAT returns through the API.

See Annex 4.A for supporting material.

Germany - New software product for electronic filing for recipients of retirement income

The German tax administration's online tax office (ELSTER) is introducing a targeted, simplified online income tax return for pensioners. This option – called "einfachELSTER" ("easy ELSTER") – is targeted towards domestic pension recipients who do not receive other types of income.

By offering this new service, the German tax administration aims to help pensioners fulfil their tax obligations, and make tax return preparation as simple as possible while still complying with applicable tax law provisions and IT standards.

The einfachELSTER system does not use a specific form. Instead, it conducts an "interview" with users, asking them a small number of questions to guide them through the income tax return. These questions use easy-to-understand language that is tailored to the target group. The service is easy to use, even for inexperienced users.

The einfachELSTER system also uses a highly simplified authentication process that is not only user-friendly but also complies with high security standards.

An agile, iterative process was used to develop the einfachELSTER system. The target group was actively included in the development process – pensioners tested each development stage and evaluated interview questions and explanatory texts in terms of clarity and user-friendliness. The feedback from users helped the development team build a system that is specifically tailored to the target group.

Portugal - IVA Automático +

IVA Automático+ (pre-filling of VAT returns) is available to certain taxable persons established in Portugal. This pre-filling uses the output and input VAT values obtained from the data contained in invoices issued via the Tax Administration's web portal and also the data submitted by taxable persons through the e-invoice system. In order to assess deductible VAT correctly, the taxpayer has to classify invoices where s/he appears as the acquirer in a business activity, as well as to mention the amount of legally deductible input VAT.

This functionality is based on data from the "E-fatura" (e-invoice system), which supports the transaction based reporting obligation. Taxable persons for VAT purposes have to submit selected information to the Tax Administration regarding each document issued, mainly invoices, independently of whether they were issued in electronic format or not. This obligation applies to almost all VAT taxable persons, and other taxable persons can also issue invoices on the Tax Administration web portal.

This functionally not only represents an easier way to fulfil the VAT return obligation available to smaller taxpayers, it also facilitates the compliance and control functions of the tax administration.

See Annex 4.A for supporting material.

Singapore - Extension of No-Filing Service (NFS) to self-employed persons

From 2021, eligible commission agents and taxi/ private hire car drivers have been selected for the Inland Revenue Authority of Singapore's (IRAS) No-Filing Service (NFS). This means they would not be required to file their Income Tax Returns with IRAS unless they have taxable income which was not made known to IRAS through third parties, or if there are changes to be made to their pre-filled relief claims based on previous years' assessments.

Instead, their tax bills were computed based on pre-filled income information obtained directly from third parties from which they derived their income. A deemed amount of expenses, based on a prescribed percentage of their gross income earned, was automatically allowed against their pre-filled income.

To qualify for NFS, the commission agents and taxi/ private hire car drivers had to first have their income information transmitted to IRAS via the agencies and operators from which they derived their income. In addition, the income information received must be eligible for the Fixed Expenses Deduction Ratio (FEDR) scheme (e.g. below a certain threshold). The FEDR scheme prescribes a certain percentage of the agents' and drivers' gross income as expenses, which can be deducted against their taxable income.

About 12 000 self-employed persons benefitted from the NFS in 2021. For some, their tax payments are automatically deducted from their designated bank accounts, allowing for a fully automated and hassle-free tax filing and payment experience.

Sources: Australia (2022), Colombia (2022), Denmark (2022), Germany (2022), Portugal (2022) and Singapore (2022).

As the levels of data available to support pre-filling grows, tax administrations are able to develop predictive techniques that can spot errors that taxpayers make as they finalise their return. A growing trend is also the use of 'nudge' techniques to prompt completion of certain fields that data suggests a taxpayer should be completing. Techniques such as these are changing compliance approaches as they are reducing errors and bringing the compliance work 'upstream' into tax administration processes, bringing significant resource benefits to tax administrations. Later chapters have more detail on nudge techniques and the increasingly sophisticated use of data in compliance work.

Box 4.3. Examples – Upstream compliance

Australia – Real-time online checks

In Australia, the Online BAS Check (OBC) is designed to improve the Business Activity Statement (BAS) lodgement experience for businesses by reducing the number of inadvertent errors (such as honest mistakes, transposition, and arithmetic errors). It uses analytics and clients' historic BAS data to forecast future outcomes and produce pre-lodgement nudge messages. The messages prompt the client in real time to check the amounts entered at a label where it is higher or lower than expected, helping them to get it right and reducing the number of inadvertent errors.

By providing real-time prompts, OBC presents an opportunity for businesses to review information, self-correct any errors and avoid post-lodgement adjustments or audit.

This preventative engagement delivers benefits for businesses through:

- Reduced compliance costs for meeting their tax obligations by avoiding penalties, general interest charges and costs associated with an audit process and/or the need to amend their BAS down the track.
- Improved confidence and visibility for business cashflow due to increased accuracy of assessments.

This is expected to reduce both post-lodgement client initiated amendments and also the effort required by the tax administration to undertake compliance activity to correct these Activity Statements post-lodgement and, in some cases, post-refund.

Spain – Using behavioural insight

In 2021, the Spanish Tax Agency (AEAT) launched an innovative project during the Personal Income Tax (PIT) campaign, developing several predictive models to improve the information provided by taxpayers in their returns.

Thousands of taxpayers modify, every year, the information related to income from work provided by the pre-populated PIT return. However, a significant percentage of these modifications are erroneous. In order to tackle this issue, AEAT decided to develop machine learning models that learnt from past tax procedures, by analysing and discovering which characteristics of taxpayers, or which of their circumstances, make them more likely to make a mistake in an eventual modification of the return. By doing so, the AEAT was able to categorize taxpayers who have a higher probability of making a mistake.

The system was integrated with the AEAT application for filing personal income tax returns. Therefore, when a taxpayer tries to modify data while filing the return, if the system determines that the taxpayer has a high probability of making a mistake, a 'nudge' message will be shown, with the aim of reducing the total number of erroneous modifications. With this new approach, AEAT managed to go one step further in achieving the concept of compliance-by-design, making use of behavioural insights and analytics to try to prevent undesirable actions on the side of the taxpayer that may harm the quality of the return.

First estimates show that the use of nudge messages on taxpayer behaviour was highly effective as around 70% of taxpayers decided not to make the planned modification in the end.

See Annex 4.A for supporting material.

Sources: Australia (2022) and Spain (2022).

Figure 4.1. Third party income information used to pre-fill PIT returns or assessments, 2020

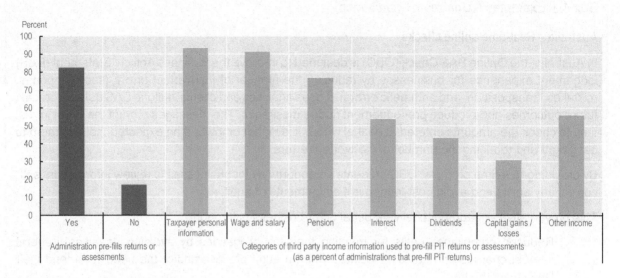

Source: Table A.42 Pre-fill of tax returns – income information.

StatLink ⬛️ᵢₗₛᴸ https://doi.org/10.1787/888934310537

Figure 4.2. Categories of tax deductible expenses used to pre-fill PIT returns or assessments, 2020

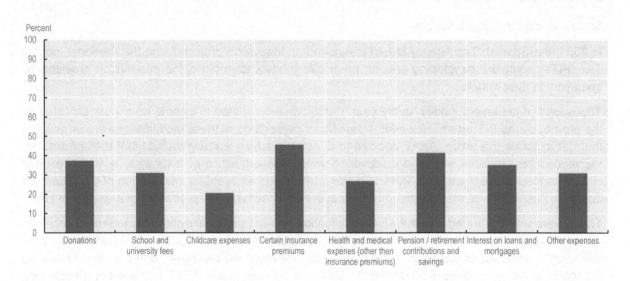

Source: Table A.43 Pre-fill of tax returns - expense information.

StatLink ⬛️ᵢₗₛᴸ https://doi.org/10.1787/888934310556

On-time return filing

Even allowing for changes occurring because of pre-filled or no-return regimes, the filing of a tax return is still the principal means by which a tax liability is established and becomes payable. As a result, the on-time filing rate is seen as an effective measure of the health of the tax system as well as the performance of the tax administration itself.

Table 4.4 summarises on-time return filing for those administrations able to supply information by tax type. Apart from CIT, the rates are around 85%. The lower rates for CIT may be explained through more complexity in the corporate income tax system and the preparation of financial statements and year-end reports.

Table 4.4. Average on-time filing rates (in percent) by tax type

Tax type	2018	2019	2020
Personal income tax (39 jurisdictions)	85.2	85.0	85.3
Corporate income tax (41 jurisdictions)	78.0	79.1	78.3
Employer withholding (28 jurisdictions)	88.9	88.0	87.2
Value added tax (44 jurisdictions)	87.0	86.3	85.8

Note: The table shows the average on-time filing rates for those jurisdictions that were able to provide the information for the years 2018, 2019 and 2020. The number of jurisdictions for which data was available is shown in parenthesis.

Table 4.5 shows the evolution of on-time filing rates. This has remained broadly static between 2014 and 2020 though it is encouraging that despite the impact of the pandemic filing rates remained stable, although Figure 4.3 shows the significant variation in on-time filing rates by tax type.

The underlying data for on-time filing also shows significant variation in on-time filing rates between jurisdictions, often reflecting that some jurisdictions had different responses to the pandemic for different tax types. The 2020 report *Tax Administration Responses to COVID-19: Measures Taken to Support Taxpayers* highlighted how some jurisdictions may have required on-time filing, for example to pay out refunds or to provide other government benefits, but allowed delayed payment, while some may have relaxed penalties for late filing (CIAT/IOTA/OECD, 2020[1]).

In the future these rates may be expected to recover and improve further as electronic filing and taxpayer services, such as pre-filling, continue to grow. It should be noted that the table only takes into account information from jurisdictions that were able to provide data for both years 2014 and 2020, which explains the differences in 2020 averages shown in Tables 4.4 and 4.5.

Table 4.5. Evolution of on-time filing rates (in percent) between 2014 and 2020 by tax type

Tax type	2014	2020	Difference in percentage points
Personal income tax (35 jurisdictions)	85.5	87.2	+1.7
Corporate income tax (36 jurisdictions)	80.2	80.9	+0.7
Employer withholding (18 jurisdictions)	86.7	88.1	+1.4
Value added tax (39 jurisdictions)	86.3 (2016)	85.9	-0.4

Note: The table shows the average on-time filing rates for those jurisdictions that were able to provide the information for the years 2014 and 2020. The number of jurisdictions for which data was available is shown in parenthesis. For VAT, the table compares information for the years 2016 and 2020, as the underlying question was changed with ISORA 2018.
Sources: Table D.12 On-time filing rates, OECD (2017), *Tax Administration 2017: Comparative Information on OECD and Other Advanced and Emerging Economies*, Table A.6, https://doi.org/10.1787/tax_admin-2017-en and OECD (2019), *Tax Administration 2019: Comparative Information on OECD and Other Advanced and Emerging Economies*, Table D.12, https://doi.org/10.1787/74d162b6-en.

Given the impact on compliance rates, many tax administrations are turning to behavioural insight techniques to try and encourage more accurate filing. This is seeing promising results, with tax administrations reporting that 'nudges' at key points in the filing process can increase the timeliness of filing. Not only is this improving compliance rates, but is also freeing up resources that can be used elsewhere.

Box 4.4. United Kingdom – Use of behavioural insight to improve filing

Despite their best efforts, some taxpayers make simple errors in calculating the tax they owe and others do not take enough care when they submit their tax returns. This, alongside other behaviours (e.g. evasion and avoidance), contributes to loss of revenue and widens the tax gap.

To address this, Her Majesty's Revenue and Customs (HMRC) has piloted the use of error prevention prompts in its online platforms to help customers avoid making common errors as they file their tax returns. The error prevention prompts appear in places where common errors can occur giving customers a chance to reflect on their entries before they are submitted. These digital prompts provide timely support to customers by directing their attention to key information as they are filling out their tax returns. This helps to build their tax literacy, helping them to get tax right, first time. By intervening early, this also helps to avoid the need for costly compliance interventions. Research with customers shows that digital prompts helped them to understand how to proceed or provided reassurance that they were proceeding in the correct way.

As the United Kingdom moves further forward in the digitisation of tax administration, HMRC has also collaborated with third party providers to develop error prevention prompts for use in commercial software. By working with third party providers, HMRC is creating more opportunities to support customers and prevent common errors at an earlier stage in the customer journey.

Source: United Kingdom (2022).

Figure 4.3. Range in on-time filing performance across major tax types, 2020

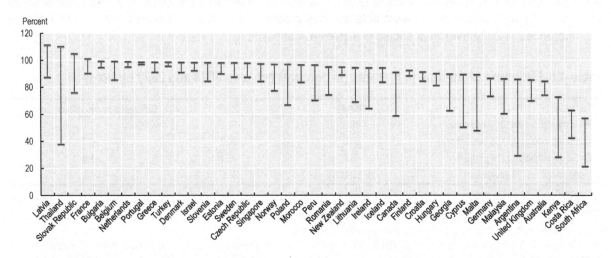

Note: On-time filing performance is expressed as a percentage of returns expected and can therefore be above 100%. The figure shows for each jurisdiction the range in on-time filing performances in 2020 across the four tax types: PIT, CIT, Employer WHT and VAT (where applicable). It only includes jurisdictions for which information was available for at least three tax types.
Source: Table D.12 On-time filing rates.

StatLink https://doi.org/10.1787/888934310575

Figure 4.4. PIT and CIT on-time filing rates, 2020

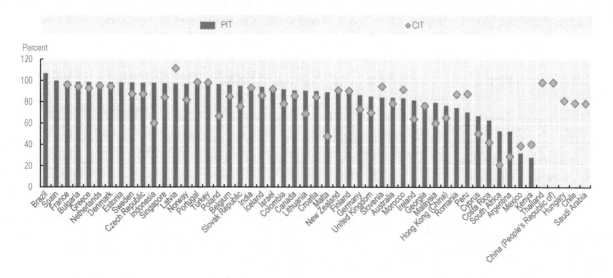

Note: On-time filing performance is expressed as a percentage of returns expected and can therefore be above 100%.
Source: Table D.12 On-time filing rates.

StatLink ᗰᓂᔕᑐ https://doi.org/10.1787/888934310594

On-time payment

Payment of tax constitutes one of the most common interactions between taxpayers and tax administrations, especially for businesses that are typically required to regularly remit a variety of payments covering both their own tax liabilities and those of their employees. Administrations continue to make progress in increasing the range of e-payment options available to taxpayers and to increase their use. This progress not only lowers the cost to the administration, it can also increase on-time payments and reduce the number of payment arrears cases by providing improved access and a better payment experience. One significant development is the growth of payment facilities being built into the natural systems of taxpayers. This is making payment more seamless for taxpayers as they can use their existing banking or accounting software to make payments.

Table 4.6. Average on-time payment rates (in percent) by tax type

Tax type	2018	2019	2020
Personal income tax (32 jurisdictions)	83.7	82.4	79.2
Corporate income tax (33 jurisdictions)	84.8	85.2	82.5
Employer withholding (28 jurisdictions)	94.9	94.8	92.3
Value added tax (33 jurisdictions)	88.3	88.4	87.4

Note: The table shows the average on-time payment rates for those jurisdictions that were able to provide the information for the years 2018, 2019 and 2020. The number of jurisdictions for which data was available is shown in parenthesis.
Source: Table D.17 On-time payment performance.

On-time payment rates for those administrations able to supply information by tax type are summarised in Tables 4.6. and 4.7. Table 4.6 shows that in 2020 on-time payment rates have fallen when compared with previous years. The range of on-time payment depicted in Figure 4.5. shows a significant gap in on-time payment across the main tax types for a number of jurisdictions, in some cases above 50 percentage points.

This reduction in on-time rates is almost certainly an impact of the pandemic, reflecting the cash flow challenges businesses and individuals may have had. It may also reflect the numerous easements some tax administrations gave on payment timeliness to assist with the challenges of the pandemic, for example where taxpayers may have been required to file on time, but had longer time to pay.

Table 4.7. Evolution of on-time payment rates (in percent) between 2014 and 2020 by tax type

Tax type	2014	2020	Difference in percentage points
Personal income tax (16 jurisdictions)	80.4	78.4	-2.0
Corporate income tax (15 jurisdictions)	89.6	86.3	-3.3
Employer withholding (15 jurisdictions)	93.4	93.0	-0.4
Value added tax (17 jurisdictions)	89.0	88.8	-0.2

Note: The table shows the average on-time filing rates for those jurisdictions that were able to provide the information for the years 2014 and 2019. The number of jurisdictions for which data was available is shown in parenthesis. Data for Costa Rica has been excluded from the calculations for PIT, CIT and VAT as it would distort the average ratios.
Sources: Table D.17 On-time payment performance and OECD (2017), *Tax Administration 2017: Comparative Information on OECD and Other Advanced and Emerging Economies*, Table A.9, https://doi.org/10.1787/tax_admin-2017-en.

Future editions of this report will track these trends, and recovering and increasing on-time payment rates should continue be an area of focus for administrations given the amounts of revenue involved. This is why some tax administrations report investing resources in this area, as can be seen in the examples in Box 4.5.

Box 4.5. Examples – Increasing on-time filing and payment

Hungary – Increasing on-time VAT filing

In view of the fact that the highest budget revenue is generated by VAT and the reduction of the VAT tax gap is of core importance, the central risk analysis unit of the National Tax and Customs Administration has initiated the development of an individual taxpayer risk model.

The purpose of the model is to anticipate changes in taxpayer behaviour at the time of submitting the tax return. It was assumed that by addressing this problem earlier, compliance can be maintained at higher levels.

To start, risk analysts collected tax administration data and information that could characterise this form of behaviour. During the work, professional and behavioural variables were developed, based on the data of taxpayers' employees, online invoicing, cash register operation, current account and representation data. Additional variables were set up based on the taxpayers' tax return habits, and a software analysis determined the strength of the indicators used to explain whether the taxpayer is significantly late or completely fails to submit the VAT return. From these parameters, the model could "learn" about the relevant behavioural characteristics of the group.

Based on preliminary results, the models have significant prediction power in identifying the behaviour of taxpayers.

See Annex 4.A for supporting material.

Singapore - Expanding e-payment options

In collaboration with a local bank, IRAS integrated its payment Application Programming Interface (API) with the bank's digital mobile banking platform – to enable taxpayers to view and pay their income tax

---

and property tax easily. This app made financial planning more inclusive and accessible, while recognising tax as an integral part of the financial planning process.

The app allows taxpayers to access the breakdown of their yearly assessable income, information of their property, their outstanding income and property tax balances, and their current financial holdings. This overview helps users easily work out their budget, income and expenses, including any upcoming tax payments. It also serves to remind taxpayers to pay their taxes promptly, thus avoiding missing payment deadlines and unnecessary penalties.

This solution also eases a common pain-point among taxpayers, who traditionally had to switch between different platforms to view their outstanding tax details and make tax payments. The integration with IRAS' APIs allows taxpayers to pay the correct amount of tax and the pre-population of the necessary information reduces any data entry errors by the taxpayers when making payment to IRAS. For IRAS, payments received are updated into the ledgers expeditiously and accurately.

Within 3 months from the launch of the bank's app, 70% of the bank's customers who used to pay their taxes via the Bank's online bill payment channels converted to using the app to access their tax details and make their tax payments.

Spain – Integrating online payments

The Online NRC (Número de Referencia completo/Full Reference Number) is an IT tool developed to immediately transfer to the AEAT databases information about online payments made by taxpayers to settle their tax bills.

The NRC is a 22-character alphanumeric code that incorporates the basic information of the payment in encrypted form, (Taxpayer's National ID, tax return, period, amount) in such a way that guarantees both its own authenticity and the receipt on which it is recorded.

Prior to this new development, the information on payments made by taxpayers was sent to AEAT in two ways. The first from the information that banks send to the tax administration on a bimonthly basis, and the second as a result of the justification of payment presented by the taxpayer in the course of a tax procedure.

This new development will allow AEAT to solve, almost in real time, those cases in which taxpayers request certain actions (refund, lifting of seizures, issuance of certificates of income or of being up to date with tax obligations) that are conditional upon prior payment. Consequently, this new development provides two main advantages:

- It allows better services to be provided to citizens by reducing their physical presence in the offices, avoiding unnecessary trips.
- It speeds up recovery proceedings, thanks to the immediacy of the available payment information.

See Annex 4.A for supporting material.

United Kingdom - Open Banking

HMRC offers customers a world leading Open Banking payment service, where HMRC provides a secure, efficient, and seamless single journey for our customers to pay tax that is due. This means the Open Banking Service Provider connects directly to the customer's bank and initiates an authorised payment to be sent to HMRC, reducing significantly the opportunity for error and fraud.

This new service differs from traditional bank transfer journeys which require the customer to manually input all the data needed to make a payment - such as bank sort code, account number and customer reference number - or rely on banking software which could hold out-of-date details. The new service uses HMRC's systems to prepopulate the customer's payment details automatically, so customers are reassured that the HMRC bank account details, as well as the customer reference, are correct and their liability will be updated to show they have made the payment.

In the first year that HMRC introduced the service, HMRC received over 2 million payments to the value of GBP 5 billion. Over 500 000 of these were received for Income Tax Self Assessment alone in the peak month of January.

In addition to benefitting HMRC's customers, HMRC reduced its payment processing costs and reduced the numbers of payments requiring manually resourced intervention to allocate the correct account.

Sources: Hungary (2022), Singapore (2022), Spain (2022) and the United Kingdom (2022).

Figure 4.5. Range in on-time payment performance, 2020

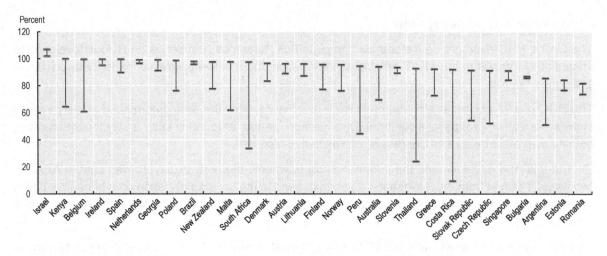

Note: On-time payments are expressed as a percentage of estimated payments expected by due date and can therefore be above 100%. The figure shows for each jurisdiction the range in on-time payment performances in 2020 across the four tax types: PIT, CIT, Employer WHT and VAT (where applicable). It only includes jurisdictions for which information was available for at least three tax types.
Source: D.17 On-time payment performance.

StatLink 🔗 https://doi.org/10.1787/888934310613

Refunds and credits

Given the underlying design of the major taxes administered (i.e. PIT, CIT and VAT), some element of over-payment by a proportion of taxpayers is unavoidable. Excess tax payments represent a cost to taxpayers in terms of "the opportunity cost", which is particularly critical to businesses that are operating with tight margins where cash flow is paramount. Any delays in refunding legitimately overpaid taxes may therefore result in significant "costs" to taxpayers.

Table 4.8. shows the different treatment of VAT refunds, and highlights that some administrations pay out refunds immediately. This is helpful to business but tax administrations need to continue to be cognisant of fraud risks. Tax regimes with a high incidence of tax refunds are particularly attractive to fraudsters (especially via organised criminal attacks) necessitating effective risk-based approaches for identifying potentially fraudulent refund claims.

During the COVID-19 crisis, the importance of paying out refunds quickly was a key issue for many governments, as a significant number of taxpayers were facing severe cash-flow problems. Tax administrations responded to this by prioritising refund applications or adapting refund processes, in some cases fully automating them. (CIAT/IOTA/OECD, 2020[11]) As economies emerge from the pandemic, the swift payment of refunds remains a priority for many governments.

Table 4.8. Treatment of VAT refunds, 2020

Percent of jurisdictions were …			
VAT refunds are automatically paid out immediately	VAT refunds are paid out immediately subject to the availability of funds	VAT refund are established as a 'credit' in the taxpayer's account, until such time as the taxpayer may legally request the refund	VAT refund are established as a 'credit' in the taxpayer's account, until such time as the taxpayer may legally request the refund, subject to the availability of funds
57%	4%	37%	2%

Source: Table A.30 VAT refunds.

The learning from both the pandemic and previous approaches is now being combined with advances in technology, and the growth of data science to provide tax administrations with new options to mitigate risks and simplify processes. This can lead to reduced administrative and compliance burdens, and the creation of new innovative approaches which can be seen in the examples in Box 4.6.

Box 4.6. Examples - Refunds and credits

Ireland - Real Time Credits

Real Time Credits is a new facility introduced for employees and pension recipients in 2021 in line with Revenue's strategy of "right tax at right time". Real Time Credits allows customers to claim as the expense is incurred, rather than at the end of the year through their tax return.

Where a customer has incurred the qualifying expenditure they can claim immediately through Revenue's secure online service and must upload a receipt with their claim ensuring compliance by design. The customer's tax calculation is adjusted in real-time to reflect the expense incurred. To give the customer the benefit of claiming their credit in real-time an instruction is made available to the payroll software of that customer's employer. The employer uses this instruction in payroll for the employee enabling a seamless real-time approach. Any resulting refund will be accounted for by the employer in the next payroll run.

Customers can claim tax relief as they incur qualifying expenditure. This means that they benefit immediately. Prior to the introduction of Real Time Credits, customers could only claim after the tax year ended and did not get the tax relief when the expense was incurred.

The introduction of Real Time Credits will result in significantly less pressure on resources at peak times as customers will be able to claim at any stage during the year. Launched in July 2021, over 11 700 claims where made up to the end of that year using this facility.

Spain - Agreement to the PIT refund proposal

Every year many euros have to be refunded to individuals as a result of the PIT campaign. Refunds are a target of the verification procedures of the Tax Agency and, although automated procedures for cross-checking and producing an assessment proposal are applied, the formalities to be followed are time

---

and resource heavy both for taxpayers and the Tax Agency. In this context, a more agile procedure has been implemented in the fiscal year 2020. In short, under this procedure:

- The Tax Agency applies its automated cross-checking procedures to detect discrepancies with the requested refund.
- Notifications are then issued in large numbers to taxpayers with discrepancies, with a proposal of reduction of the PIT refund. There is a deadline of 15 days to respond, with taxpayers either:
  - Agreeing with the proposal, in which case a receipt is automatically issued and incorporated to the taxpayer's electronic file. This speeds up the refund processing. Taxpayers can confirm their agreement online or by phone and have the agreement recorded by a tax official.
  - Disagreeing, in which case they can challenge the assessment and the regular procedure is followed.

This automation of the process has reduced the average processing time of the procedure by 15 days, which has had a direct impact in the time to get the refunds by taxpayers.

See Annex 4.A for supporting material.

Sources: Ireland (2022) and Spain (2022).

References

CIAT/IOTA/OECD (2020), *"Tax administration responses to COVID-19: Measures taken to support taxpayers", OECD Policy Responses to Coronavirus (COVID-19)*, OECD Publishing, Paris, https://doi.org/10.1787/adc84188-en. [1]

OECD (2019), *Tax Administration 2019: Comparative Information on OECD and other Advanced and Emerging Economies*, OECD Publishing, Paris, https://doi.org/10.1787/74d162b6-en. [3]

OECD (2017), *Tax Administration 2017: Comparative Information on OECD and Other Advanced and Emerging Economies*, OECD Publishing, Paris, https://doi.org/10.1787/tax_admin-2017-en. [2]

Annex 4.A. Links to supporting material (accessed on 13 May 2022)

- Box 4.1. – India: Link to document with more detail on IEC 2.0: https://www.oecd.org/tax/forum-on-tax-administration/database/b.4.1-india-iec-2.0.pdf

- Box 4.1. – Japan: Link to a presentation providing more detail on the co-operation between national and local tax offices regarding the e-filing of corporation tax returns: https://www.oecd.org/tax/forum-on-tax-administration/database/b.4.1-japan-e-filing-cit.pdf

- Box 4.2. – Denmark: Link to more detail on the code used in providing the web services: https://github.com/skat/rsu-b2b-sample-client-java

- Box 4.2. – Portugal: Links to a brochure and video explaining more about the service of pre-filling of VAT returns:
  - Brochure (in Portuguese): https://www.oecd.org/tax/forum-on-tax-administration/database/b.4.2-portugal-brochure-iva-automatico.pdf
  - Video (in Portuguese): https://www.youtube.com/watch?v=xWcldpAJhlg

- Box 4.3. – Spain: Links to presentations with more detail on the use of behavioural insights during the PIT campaign:
  - https://www.oecd.org/tax/forum-on-tax-administration/database/b.4.3-spain-using-behavioural-insight-eng.pdf (English short version); and
  - https://www.oecd.org/tax/forum-on-tax-administration/database/b.4.3-spain-using-behavioural-insight-esp.pdf (Spanish comprehensive version).

- Box 4.5. – Hungary: Links to a document and video containing more detail on the model developed to anticipate changes in taxpayer behaviour:
  - Document: https://www.oecd.org/tax/forum-on-tax-administration/database/b.4.5-hungary-predictive-modelling-of-vat.pdf; and
  - Video: https://www.youtube.com/watch?v=zviwtbPF6AI

- Box 4.5. – Spain: Links to a document and websites containing more detail on the IT tool developed to immediately transfer to the administration information about online payments made by taxpayers:
  - Document: https://www.oecd.org/tax/forum-on-tax-administration/database/b.4.5-spain-online-nrc.pdf
  - Websites (in Spanish):
    - https://sede.agenciatributaria.gob.es/Sede/ayuda/consultas-informaticas/pago-impuestos-deudas-tasas-ayuda-tecnica/que-nrc.html
    - https://sede.agenciatributaria.gob.es/Sede/ayuda/consultas-informaticas/pago-impuestos-deudas-tasas-ayuda-tecnica/pago-autoliquidaciones.html

- Box 4.6. – Spain: Links to:
  - A screenshot of the taxpayer view of a PIT return in the Tax Agency´s electronic office where the two possibilities (agreement or disagreement) are offered: https://www.oecd.org/tax/forum-on-tax-administration/database/b.4.6-spain-screenshot-taxpayer-view-on-online-pit-return.pdf (English text added as a courtesy); and
  - The model template of the receipt of the agreement: https://www.oecd.org/tax/forum-on-tax-administration/database/b.4.6-spain-model-template-of-receipt-of-agreement.pdf (English text added as a courtesy).

5 Services

This chapter considers how tax administrations' compliance goals are enhanced by providing effective and efficient services to taxpayers, often through technology. This is helping increase compliance amongst taxpayers by making it easier to understand tax obligations, report taxable income and make payments.

Introduction

A central element in supporting taxpayer compliance is the provision of a wide range effective and easy to use taxpayer services. Many of these services centre on communication channels, both on a reactive and proactive basis. Often, these communications have been delivered on a one-to-many basis, such as the provision of guidance or reminders as well as calculation and reporting tools. However, tax administrations report that their use of innovative tools is growing, and those tools are also allowing communications to become more personalised to the taxpayer's individual circumstances, to be delivered via an increasing range of communication channels and to facilitate the drive towards self-service, on a real-time and 24/7 basis. Some like India have invested in specific communication centres where sound proofed live interactions between the income tax department and other stakeholders like taxpayers, tax practitioners, experts, and policy makers are possible, and can also be streamed on social media channels where appropriate.

In addition, tax administrations are reporting a rapid growth in the use of technology to transform their operational models. The use of advanced techniques in artificial intelligence, machine learning and machine to machine links are opening up new service options for tax administrations that allow more 'compliance-by-design' style approaches to be made available. This is a growing trend that is expected to accelerate as tax administrations continue to unlock the power of digital transformation.

Behavioural insights

The growth in the use of technology has often been supported by a growth in the use of behavioural insights. Behavioural insights is an interdisciplinary field of research using principles from the behavioural sciences such as psychology, neuroscience, and behavioural economics to understand how individuals absorb, process, and react to information. These principles can be used to design practical policies and interventions based on human behaviour. This can be particularly powerful when combined with insights gathered from the analysis of the increasingly large volumes of data available to tax administration, both internally and externally generated.

Previous editions of this series have seen and increasing number of tax administrations report employing behavioural researchers and using behavioural insights in specific areas to influence voluntary compliance. This trend has continued with close to 70% of administrations reporting the use of behavioural insight methodologies or techniques in 2020 (see Figure 6.1). Chapter 10 of the 2019 edition of this report contains further insight into these developments. This trend has continued, with behavioural insights being increasingly mainstreamed into wider tax administration strategies and interventions. The 2021 report from the OECD's FTA Behavioural Insight Community of Interest also contains many examples of this in practice (OECD, 2021[1]).

Box 5.1. Examples - Behavioural insights

Brazil - Behavioural analysis

The Behavioural Insights Project started with a test over 2 489 small companies that earned more during the pandemic than in previous years in order to prompt compliant behaviour. In this test, there were 3 different letters, each using a different behavioural science technique and a control of the existing letter. The tests were Social Norms, Social Norms plus Simplification, Loss Aversion plus Consequences.

The letters with behavioural insights worked better than the current models in around 8% of cases. However, when groups are stratified into smaller universes according to their tax evasion risk profile, they responded differently. The high tax risk taxpayers responded worse to all the test letters than they did to traditional communication by over 8%. In contrast, the medium and moderate tax risk groups responded to a letter focused on social norms and simplification with improvements of around 31% and 15%, respectively. Finally, the low tax risk group responded better to a letter focused on loss aversion by around 41%.

Following this there was a second test where a letter focused on reminders and appointments worked better for taxpayers with smaller debts, while letters focused on social norms and loss aversion worked better for taxpayers with higher debts.

The learning is that the inclusion of behavioural prompts in letters sent to taxpayers makes a difference, with the result depending on taxpayer profiles. As a result there is a now an artificial intelligence study to predict the appropriate choice of letter for each taxpayer.

Ireland - Prompt for Action Development

Ireland has developed a system to use a high degree of personalisation to nudge taxpayers to meet their obligations. This builds on the capability to communicate efficiently with customers and encouraging them to use Revenue's online services and portals to ensure they pay the right tax at the right time.

In order to get real time feedback from customers a proof of concept was undertaken. This involved targeting a limited cohort of e-enabled customers. Using defined criteria to select these specific customers, highly personalised messages were sent through Revenue's online system.

The scope of the development is to create a seamless communications process with selected cohorts. The result is a personalised communication containing a range of information and data specific to each customer, requesting them to complete an action. The provision of personal information prompts more interaction from the customer.

The tailored communication also prompts the customer to take the precise actions that are required of them to engage with Revenue efficiently using online systems, enhancing their customer service interaction, thus developing the customers understanding of their tax treatment and obligations for effective compliance.

The facility will enhance Revenue's business operational processes and will allow business areas to streamline the selection process to accurately identify and target cohorts for bulk personalised outputs.

United Kingdom - Using behavioural insights to improve timeliness

In a typical year, the majority of Self-Assessment (SA) customers file their returns in January. In 2021-22, Her Majesty's Revenue and Customs (HMRC) wanted to encourage early filing to break the habit of filing later, as well as reminding those that have filed early before to continue doing so.

Qualitative and quantitative research on SA filing in 2013 found that customers report the following reasons for filing later:

- Personal circumstances: adversity, disorganisation, financial difficulty
- Ability, awareness, and engagement
- Fear of making errors and mistrust towards HMRC
- Complexity e.g. some customers do not understand that 'filing' is different to 'paying'
- Customer experience e.g. customers might be reluctant to turn to HMRC if they have not previously got the help they needed.

> SA customers tend to need multiple reminders, so we used as many channels as possible, presenting information in a clear and easy to navigate format to make information easier to understand and action. This included a factsheet on the UK government website, letters, emails, media, social media and stakeholder engagement.
>
> An example of this was a new email reminder in May 2021 which focused on the help and support available to customers to file their return. This led to a 7% increase in early filing (13 000 more people filed within 60 days) and about 3% more customers, who previously filed early, continued to file early. There was no increase in inbound call rates.
>
> Sources: Brazil (2022), Ireland (2022), and the United Kingdom (2022).

Managing service demand

An important aspect of meeting taxpayer preferences is getting the mix of channels right. While there is an increasing shift to the use of electronic services for both convenience and cost-efficiency purposes, a proportion of taxpayers will not have access to, or be comfortable with such services. This calls for considered strategies as to how to influence channel shift for those for whom it would offer better outcomes without adversely affecting the service offering to other taxpayers.

Such strategies of course need to be based on good measurement and understanding of demands and constraints. Table 5.1 highlights the shift to digital that occurred during the pandemic, with use of online channels growing significantly. This is against a rapid decline in the use of traditional channels (in-person and paper). Interestingly the volume of telephone calls did not rise significantly during the pandemic, suggesting that digital channels were effective at meeting taxpayer demands. It will be interesting to track service demand by channel in future editions of this report, to assess if the pandemic has caused a structural shift.

Table 5.1. Service demand by channel

Channel type	No. of jurisdictions providing data	2018	2019	2020	Change 2018-19	Change 2019-20
Online via taxpayer account	31	847 480 869	1 011 407 743	1 286 851 433	+19.3%	+27.2%
Telephone call	52	328 816 038	314 207 157	329 807 813	-4.4%	+5.0%
In-person	35	109 620 990	109 620 990	48 699 279	-0.5%	-55.3%
Mail / post	18	35 045 875	35 167 199	32 219 102	+0.3%	-8.4%
E-mail	29	12 424 490	13 846 716	19 077 219	+11.4%	+37.8%
Digital assistance	28	10 478 405	21 218 519	30 728 014	+102.5%	+44.8%

Note: The table only includes jurisdictions for which data was available for 2018, 2019 and 2020.
Source: Table A.40 Incoming service contacts: Monitoring and number of contacts by channel (online, digital assistance, telephone) and Table A.41 Incoming service contacts: Number of contacts by channel (e-mail, mail / post, in-person).

Supporting self-service

As highlighted earlier, the self-service offering from tax administrations continues to grow, and there is an expanding range of self-services being provided. Common examples of this include the ability to register, file and pay on-line, along with a range of interactive tools. This is leading to efficiency gains in tax administrations, as well as being able to provide a more 24/7-style service to taxpayers. These services proved to be invaluable during the COVID-19 pandemic. A number of tax administrations are also applying artificial intelligence techniques to the large amounts of data that is collected through these services to help develop them further to better meet taxpayers' needs. Chapter 6 also sets out how these large amounts of data are being used in audit work.

Box 5.2. Examples – Developments in self-service

Chile – Taxpayer reports

The taxpayer report is an initiative implemented in Chile in 2020, to promote the accountability of public expenditure. The objective is that people know the amounts they have paid, the specific contribution they have made through the payment of their taxes, and how these resources have been allocated to meet the needs of the country. This should increase the transparency of the tax administration and the State. This report is tailor-made for each taxpayer whose income information is available, in the months of April-May of each year, and has 3 sections:

- 'How much did I contribute through taxes?' shows information on the taxes paid the previous year, across income tax, and has an estimate of the VAT and immovable property tax amounts.
- 'How were my taxes spent?' shows a disaggregation of the tax paid by type and area of public spending, indicating how much was spent in education, health, social protection, and so on.
- 'Total income and public spending' shows the state of the public finances indicating the income received in the previous year and the total public spending.

For citizens where a report is not possible, they can access a calculator of taxes and public expenses, in which a similar report is generated after the taxpayer submits an estimate of their monthly income.

See Annex 5.A for supporting material.

China (People's Republic of) - Digital tax accounts

The State Tax Administration (STA) has built an electronic taxation bureau for individual taxpayers that fits with the new individual income tax system and the new tax collection and administration model for individual taxpayers, whose design concept is very similar to that mentioned in the OECD's Tax Administration 3.0 report (OECD, 2020[2]).

Digital tax accounts for individual taxpayers across the People's Republic of China have been established with secure digital identification capabilities, that includes a taxpayer identification number for individual taxpayers. This means the largest tax-related digital service channel has been set up for precise and real-time online interaction between tax administrations and hundreds of millions of taxpayers.

In the individual digital tax accounts, new business rules covering the whole process of individual income tax meaning the automatic operation of taxation business and the intelligent provision of service and management are driven by "data plus rules".

The digital tax accounts for individual taxpayers also provide intelligent accounting and tax calculation services for individual taxpayers, which promotes self-service among individual taxpayers, and further enhances tax collection and administration. In the annual reconciliation of the comprehensive income of individual income tax in 2020, more than 98% of individual taxpayers have enjoyed pre-filling services in the declaration form, which has significantly reduced the difficulty of tax filing and improved efficiency.

Czech Republic - Modern and Easy Taxes project

In the Czech Republic there are continuous efforts to simplify the administration of taxes and improve communication between the Tax Administration and the taxpayer. As a result of these efforts "MOJE daně" (My Taxes) project was introduced and launched at the end of February 2021. The shortcut "MOJE" stands for modern (MOderní) and easy (JEdnoduché) taxes in English and expresses the client centric approach of Tax Administration. The service is available to both individuals as well as legal entities.

An online tax office "My Taxes" offers a 24/7 access to taxpayers allowing them to view their tax liabilities, tax returns, tax forms or to file a tax return online from anywhere. The "My Taxes" portal also features other tools which make tax compliance easier such as prefilled basic data (e.g. name and address) in tax returns, alerts regarding the due date of a tax liability, or to warn taxpayers that the tax account has an unpaid balance.

To log in to "My Taxes" portal taxpayers can use various methods, e.g. an e-identity from an ID card with an electronic chip, a bank identity, or via a Tax Office.

Hungary - Development and services of the new Customer Portal

Renewing the web portal to reduce the administrative burden for taxpayers and to increase the customer satisfaction index, was one of the major development areas of the National Tax and Customs Administration (NTCA). This lead to a new portal with a consistent look that offered a higher level of service, is easy to use for different taxpayer groups, i.e. citizens and businesses, and has a modern search function. The responsive design of the portal works across a range of devices and can be customised according to the user's needs and is fully accessible.

After logging in, the client can access the personal client profile prepared by the tax administration and representatives can access the personal profiles of their clients. The profile includes, personal data, net balance of the current account, missing declarations and a personal tax calendar.

The portal also provides direct access to the online form filling service and to the interactive, intelligent filing interface of the personal income tax return. If there are arrears, the client can settle the payment obligation by means of an online payment. If there are refunds due, the client can offset them against other liabilities. Numerous other services are available through the portal, including the booking system for customer services, and the Online Invoice data.

See Annex 5.A for supporting material.

India - Compliance Portal

The Compliance Portal aims to deliver seamless communication and is part of the voluntary compliance management framework in India. It enables seamless two-way structured communication that can enhance the transparency and functional efficiency of the tax administration.

The Compliance Portal displays taxpayer information through an Annual Information Statement (AIS). The AIS shows information received from various sources on the taxpayer so that the taxpayer can correct the information as required. In case of incorrect information, the Compliance Portal also provides the functionality for supplying the correct information. The information available in the AIS is also utilised for pre-filling the Income tax return, which simplifies and eases the process of return filing. The Compliance Portal is part of the Graded Compliance Management Framework which enables the taxpayer to fill potential compliance gaps before the information is utilised by the tax administration for risk management. For taxpayers where the profile and the tax returns do not match with the transactions, various campaigns through emails and SMS are executed and taxpayers are made aware of such information being available with the department, and are given the facility to correct such information.

The Compliance Portal is backed by a dedicated Compliance Management Central Processing Centre which acts as an operational centre for the Portal. It also performs the function of a helpdesk for providing assistance and resolving any issues that the taxpayer might have in respect of the Compliance Portal.

Japan - Tax return portal website

The Japanese government has assigned a 12-digit number known as "My Number" to every resident in Japan to support social security or taxation procedures. After the assignment and notification to a resident of My Number, a "My Number Card" can be issued upon request from the Japanese resident. My Number Card enables the Japanese residents to complete some administrative procedures including taxation matters online, which has increased administrative efficiency and reduced burdens.

Since October 2020, My Number Card holders have been able to declare tax returns online through "Mynaportal". Mynaportal automatically inputs the amount of the insurance premiums they paid in the previous year to the tax declarations and conducts year-end adjustments. The number of taxpayers who used this system in 2020 is 2.51 million. Japan has encouraged taxpayers to use Mynaportal instead of paper-based declarations and is also planning to develop additional functions to input other information from deduction certificates such as a certificate for income taxes etc. withheld from the national pension.

Another advantage of the My Number System is that taxpayers will no longer be required to submit a copy of their identification documents (such as a certificate of residence) during the filing procedure. Furthermore, the system allows statutory statements to be sorted based on taxpayers' My Number and thus match the statements with the tax return, helping taxpayers' income to be recognized more accurately and efficiently.

See Annex 5.A for supporting material.

Sources: Chile (2022), China (People's Republic of) (2022), the Czech Republic (2022), Hungary (2022), India (2022) and Japan (2022).

Digital assistants

The previous edition (OECD, 2021[3]) of this series highlighted how a growing number of administrations are using virtual or digital assistants to help respond to taxpayer enquiries and support self-service. As Table 5.2 shows the growth has been extremely rapid and these services are now very common. This trend was likely accelerated by the COVID-19 pandemic as these services proved to be invaluable in helping tax administrations respond to the pandemic, allowing for support to continue to be delivered to taxpayers even when services were stretched.

Table 5.2. Evolution of use of virtual assistants, artificial intelligence and application programming interfaces between 2018 and 2020

Percent of administrations that use this technology

Status of implementation and use	Virtual assistants (e.g. chatbots)			Artificial intelligence (AI), including machine learning			Application programming interfaces (APIs)		
	2018	2020	Difference in percentage points (p.p.)	2018	2020	Difference in p.p.	2018	2020	Difference in p.p.
Technology is implemented and used	34.5	60.3	+25.8	31.6	47.4	+15.8	79.0	93.0	+14.0
Technology is in the implementation phase for future use	13.8	12.1	-1.7	15.8	29.8	+14.0	7.0	7.0	±0.0
Technology is not used, incl. situations where the implementation has not started	51.7	27.6	-24.1	52.6	22.8	-29.8	14.0	0.0	-14.0

Source: Tables A.51 Innovative technologies: Implementation and usage (Part 1) and A.52 Innovative technologies: Implementation and usage (Part 2).

The success of these services are now being developed further with jurisdictions investigating how they use advances in artificial intelligence (AI) to deliver more sophisticated levels of support. Figure 5.1 shows that 40% of administrations who have a virtual assistant are using AI in some form to improve the service. This can allow the system to cope with more complex questions being asked by taxpayers and/or more personalised answers being given. This is part of the wider trend of the use of AI in tax administration which is also explored in Chapter 9.

Figure 5.1. Type of virtual assistants, 2022

Percent of administrations

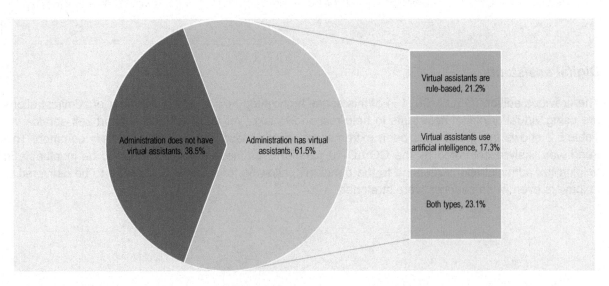

Note: The figure is based on ITTI data from 52 jurisdictions that are covered in this report and that have completed the global survey on digitalisation.
Source: OECD et al. (2022), Inventory of Tax Technology Initiatives, https://www.oecd.org/tax/forum-on-tax-administration/tax-technology-tools-and-digital-solutions/, Table TT5 (accessed on 13 May 2022).

StatLink https://doi.org/10.1787/888934310632

Box 5.3. Examples - Digital assistants

Brazil - Chatbots

Since 2021 the Federal Revenue of Brazil has offered services to the taxpayers through chatbots covering four thematic areas with six other themes in test and many others planned.

To manage budget constraints, and to prevent vendor lock in, Brazil has built its own platform, using its own hardware instead of using a commercial service provider. This also allows Brazil to gather more data on the response from taxpayers and also respond to privacy concerns. The bot engine includes a specialized language as well as a runtime and a natural language processing service based on a deep learning model. This also allows answers to be stored for future retraining.

The next stage is to create a routing chatbot to help identify the goal of the users and send them to the correct service, for example a thematic chatbot, a human-to-human chat, a video conference or to the website.

Japan - Introduction of a chatbot for tax consultation

Since October 2020, the National Tax Agency (NTA) has introduced a chat-bot to automatically provide answers to taxpayers online as a new channel of virtual tax consultation. In addition the NTA has posted answers to taxpayer's common questions on the NTA's Web site ("Tax answer"). This means in addition to the "Tax answer", taxpayers can use a chat-bot to solve their tax-related issues.

Taxpayers can ask questions concerning taxes by selecting questions from a drop down menu or by writing them in a text box, and then AI will generate answers automatically. Through using the chat-bot for tax consultations, users will be able to ask more easily questions concerning taxes at any time of the day, and access information published on the NTA website more immediately.

The NTA will continue to improve the specifications of the chatbot based on users' feedbacks and AI learnings. When the chatbot was officially introduced in 2021, the number of questions the chatbot received was 4.2 million. This has grown more than 10 fold from when the chatbot was in trial operation in 2020.

See Annex 5.A for supporting material.

Sources: Brazil (2022) and Japan (2022).

E-services

As part of the of the ongoing shift to self-service models, tax administrations report continued investment in new digital tools that can support wider goals of helping taxpayers get their tax right first time has continued. These tools provide new ways for taxpayers to interact with tax administrations, as well as helping drive the efficiencies that self-service models can deliver.

As technology has developed, the sophistication of these services has increased, with the next generation of 'intelligent' e-services starting to be developed that use artificial intelligence and to make the interactions with taxpayers more sophisticated.

Box 5.4. Examples - New e-services

Greece – myData

'myDATA' (my Digital Accounting and Tax Application) is the new electronic platform through which electronic books are introduced into the daily lives of businesses. E-Books are considered a crucial step into the digital transformation of Tax Administration that also boosts and strengthens Greek State's relationship with businesses. On 1 October 2020 the new platform was put into pilot operations and was officially introduced on 1 July 2021. In particular, myDATA monitors all transactions of Businesses' income and expenses that keep Accounting Records in accordance with Greek Accounting Standards and also it depicts their accounting and tax results.

Moreover, myDATA platform includes two types of Books:

- The Analytical (or Detailed) Book, which summarizes Company's Revenue and Expenses, classifies transactions and makes the necessary adjustments to determine each year's accounting and tax result
- The Synoptic (or Summary) Book, which summarizes company's results on a monthly and annual basis.

myDATA has more than 630 000 users, and 360 000 000 records have been transferred, with 3 million documents a day being submitted to the tax administration.

Netherlands – Automated decision transparency

The Netherlands Tax Administration (NTA) is using automated decision services extensively. These decisions are like black boxes to both civil servants and citizens, making it hard to understand the algorithms used in decision services.

Since 2015, the NTA has been working to remedy this situation by specifying rules in a controlled natural language called RegelSpraak. These rules are traceable to the source in law and policies. This allows civil servants to verify and test the rules. For citizens, the NTA is experimenting in using the rules to explain decisions. This functionality enables civil servants and ultimately tax payers to understand in detail how decisions have been made. Building on this, bad data or faulty rules can be found easily and corrected.

The NTA expects improvements in the quality of the rules both beforehand and afterward. The former because experience has shown that the need to explain something is a powerful driver for simplification. The latter because many more people can check the legality of the rules by tracing them back to their legal source. This initiative enables the NTA to push towards two strategic goals: proactively helping tax payers and being a learning organization.

Singapore - Seamless and Personalised Self-help digital services

The Inland Revenue Authority of Singapore (IRAS) has leveraged end-user automation, data and AI tools to deliver seamless and personalised taxpayer services. For example, IRAS added on a digital adoption tool to add step-by-step onscreen personalised guidance onto digital services at myTax Portal. Taking an agile approach to act on feedback as they arise, IRAS iteratively improved the guidance content and navigation for its taxpayers. During the pilot period, IRAS achieved a 13% reduction in contacts requesting for e-filing guidance and more than 86% of taxpayers surveyed found it useful in helping them to complete their digital transactions. Spurred on by these positive outcomes, IRAS has expanded usage of this approach to other digital services. IRAS is also using the data to better understand taxpayers' digital experiences within the portal. In 2021, IRAS also developed authenticated chatbot services to handle six common payment enquiries on the new Singapore Government Virtual

Intelligent Chat Assistant (VICA) platform. The VICA chatbot leverages natural language processing capabilities to provide more humanised, conversational digital experiences. Using the chatbot, taxpayers can conveniently check their outstanding tax balance, view payment plans, check payment status, cancel or reinstate payment plans and make tax payment via self-service payment terminals and mobile channels. More than 20 000 taxpayers have used these services since their launch in March 2021 and more than 75% are satisfied with the experience.

Sweden – Embedding tax rules into business systems

The Swedish Tax Agency has made significant progress in its efforts to translate tax regulations into code that can be used by business systems such as accounting software. Tax regulations and written guidance currently need to be verified manually by experts from the Swedish Tax Agency's Legal Department. However, rule-based software solutions can reduce the need for manual input, and have excellent potential for supporting and automating verification and control processes.

To facilitate compliance with the written legal guidance provided on its website, the Swedish Tax Agency is developing machine-readable rules – known as "rule bases" – which are structured to reflect the logic of tax regulations.

The aim is to enable external software developers working with business systems to create rule-based services for certain tax categories. The Swedish Tax Agency will provide software developers with APIs that include machine-readable, version-managed rule bases relating to a variety of tax categories.

The development process consists of the following steps:

- Tax experts in the Swedish Tax Agency's Legal Department develop decision trees and import them into a software program for creating rule bases.
- Rule bases are tested and verified using a rule engine.
- Rule bases are then embedded into APIs. An API includes all versions of the relevant rule set; links to human-readable versions of the same data; and content cards providing definitions, and legal explanations.

United States – Using automation to improve call centres

The Internal Revenue Service (IRS) implemented the ability for taxpayers to request a call back rather than waiting on hold, the ability for taxpayers to communicate with an assistor via text chat (and to upload account specific documents), and English and Spanish speaking voice and chat "bots" that can answer frequently asked questions, give answers about taxpayer notices, and help taxpayers with information on how to make payments. Voice bots are software powered by AI that allow a caller to navigate an interactive voice response system with their voice, generally using natural language. Taxpayers who request to speak with a customer service representative will be placed in the queue for English or Spanish telephone assistance regarding collection matters.

Chat bots simulate human conversation through web-based text interaction, while also using AI-powered software to respond to natural language prompts. The bots are currently unauthenticated, meaning they cannot answer questions about a specific taxpayer account. The IRS is working toward launching more advanced authenticated bots that would allow access to taxpayers' IRS accounts and be able to set up taxpayer-specific instalment agreements.

The goal of these bots is to improve the level of service offered to taxpayers by providing self-help options without having to wait in long queues, thereby also freeing up IRS telephone assistors to answer calls on more complex issues.

Sources: Greece (2022), the Netherlands (2022), Singapore (2022), Sweden (2022) and the United States (2022).

Mobile applications

The recent trend for the increasing use of mobile applications by tax administrations seen in other editions of this series has continued. While the main use often remains the provision of information and guidance, mobile apps are becoming increasingly transactional, and are becoming a primary way for taxpayers to access relevant records and personal tax accounts, communicate with the tax administration, supply information and tax returns and make payments. As the sophistication and availability of mobile technology has grown, the benefits of digital transformation to tax administrations in less developed administrations, where fixed line internet can be less common, has opened up. This is allowing these jurisdictions, who are often free of legacy digital systems, to provide a platform for digital transformation.

Box 5.5. Examples - Mobile applications

Indonesia – Mobile tax office

Since 2019, the Directorate General of Taxes (DGT) has initiated the Click Call Counter (3C) programme to optimize its digital services. The first part of the programme, Click service, aims at providing Taxpayers an easier access to DGT online services. In 2021, therefore, DGT launched a mobile application that can be accessed by the public using their phones. The application is a mobile-based portal for the official website of the DGT (www.pajak.go.id).

Features on the app aim to help taxpayers comply with their obligations and reduce the need to visit tax offices. Through the app taxpayers can complete a range of tasks including generating tax codes and certificates, getting status checks and updating their records, and can use a tax calendar that reminds important dates. For SMEs there is the ability to perform bookkeeping tasks such as recording daily income and completing monthly tax billing.

Italy – E-invoicing app

Electronic invoicing in Italy became mandatory in public procurement for central government administrations from 6 June 2014, and from 31 March 2015 for local government administrations. Thus, it is mandatory for all business-to-government transactions from 2015 In 2019 this was extended to transactions between businesses and private individuals. The aim of this extension is to tackle evasion and fraud, and since its introduction there has been a significant increase in VAT-related tax revenue.

In order to support economic operators, the Italian Revenue Agency (IRA) offers some free tools in addition to those available on the market. These include the mobile App called "FatturAE" which allows users to create an electronic invoice and send it through the Exchange System to the recipient. Moreover, other support features, such as a predefined templates, are provided by the App allowing the easy creation of electronic invoices, helping to minimize the risks of formal errors.

The App FatturAE was made available in 2019. Since then, about 30 000 e-invoices have been transmitted through FatturAE per year.

See Annex 5.A for supporting material.

Kenya – Mobile service strategies

M-Service is the umbrella term used to group all mobile technologies used in the delivery of Kenya Revenue Authority (KRA) services. The first implementation of M-Service was undertaken in 2013, with the overall objective of setting up a communication and mobile payment channel, through which taxpayers could query and receive information from KRA, as well as remit payments via mobile channels such as mobile wallets, mobile banking and internet banking.

The next phase of development emphasized leveraging of new technology to transform and enhance revenue mobilization, broaden the taxpayer base and raise customer satisfaction. A mobile app was identified as one of the possible channels that could deliver MService enhancement initiatives. The objectives for this work was to: establish mobile as a new channel for taxpayer engagement; to increase the speed at which mobile services can be deployed; to use a channel that is more relevant to taxpayers; and to engage previously unreachable taxpayers through mobile. This was not an easy challenge as it required alteration of existing laws, and some tax officers were resistant to the change, potentially driven by a lack of technical skills, particularly mobile technology development and security.

Once these challenges were overcome, the app has expanded the tax base with 23 000 Kenyans registered as new taxpayers on the Mobile platform in 2020/2021. Furthermore, compliance has increased with more than 14 000 taxpayers applying for a tax compliance certificate and 73 000 filing their nil returns.

Malaysia – Mytax

MyTax is one of the initiatives under the Hasil Transformation Project by Inland Revenue Board of Malaysia (IRBM). Its aim is to provide a one-stop centre of tax information for taxpayers, through a mobile website and mobile applications. MyTax is also the main channel for taxpayers to file their annual electronic forms for taxation and reliefs.

The system was developed in six months, and opened to the public on 1 November 2020. The crucial part of MyTax was the presentation of its user experience and interface so that it was easy to use by the public. Web responsive design is utilised in MyTax to provide users with full functions irrespective of the devices and user's behaviour or environment. Security was also important and MyTax is secured by Public Key Infrastructure for secure internet encryption and authentication for taxpayers.

As of 30 November 2021, there are 2 681 767 visitors to MyTax, and it is projected that the users will grow exponentially once the tax filing season starts in March 2022. MyTax is also available in the mobile app through three different platforms, and is still being enhanced further. Modules from the new Hasil Integrated Tax System are being tested for integration with MyTax, allowing e-Registration, e-Updates and other e-applications. Taxpayers can also submit their Income Remittance by uploading data, which will be prefilled in their oncoming tax filing. Furthermore, MyTax will continue to be integrated with other systems such as e-Filing, and the Revenue Management System, geolocation functions, online registration verification for taxpayers, uploading and downloading e-documents.

See Annex 5.A for supporting material.

Sources: Indonesia (2022), Italy (2022), Kenya (2022) and Malaysia (2022).

Non-digital services

Digital services have been critical to tax administrations delivering enhanced services to customers, as well as opening up new service options. As digital services have grown, tax administrations are increasingly aware that some groups may not have access to digital services, or may not be comfortable with them. Figure 5.2 highlights that 80% of administrations offer specific services to support those who are not online, and over 60% make sure their services are available to those with a disability. Whilst more progress clearly needs to be made in this space, these programmes are starting to ensure that all taxpayers are served effectively by the tax administration. Tax administrations are therefore continuing to invest in detailed research to understanding the needs and drivers of these taxpayers groups and to develop considered strategies as to how to serve these taxpayers in the most appropriate way.

Figure 5.2. Non-digital services and services for users with visual, auditory, motor or cognitive disabilities, 2022

Percent of administrations

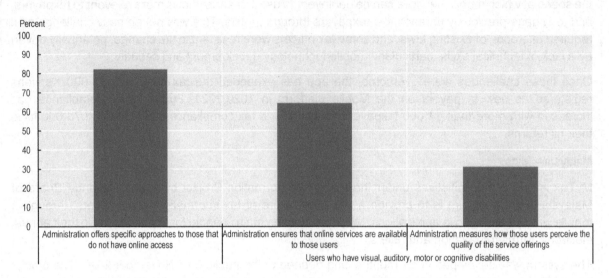

Note: The figure is based on ITTI data from 52 jurisdictions that are covered in this report and that have completed the global survey on digitalisation
Source: OECD et al. (2022), Inventory of Tax Technology Initiatives, https://www.oecd.org/tax/forum-on-tax-administration/tax-technology-tools-and-digital-solutions/, Table TT4 (accessed on 13 May 2022).

StatLink ⬛ᐧᔑ⬛ https://doi.org/10.1787/888934310651

Box 5.6. Ireland - Analysis to identify taxpayer service needs and trends

Each year Revenue deals with high volumes of customer contacts by phone, email and post, which requires a significant human resource to manage. In a bid to identify customer pain points and devise strategies to address them effectively, a project was undertaken to analyse customer contacts for 'self-assessed' customers over a 12-month period.

Revenue's Data Analytics team provided high-level data of customer contacts which was segmented, including by customer age groupings. This revealed high multi-contact volume levels (five or more in a 12-month period) for older (age 65+) self-assessed customers. A deep-dive analysis of the individual customer contacts was undertaken to critically evaluate our service offering.

From the pain points identified the customers were found to be very compliant. However they were also found to require high levels of support in completing tax returns, high levels of 'reassurance' that they had completed tax returns correctly, and many were potentially filing tax returns unnecessarily.

A range of strategies were devised and piloted (without being advertised) to address the issues identified, this included:

- Providing a dedicated phone service for this customer cohort, noting many were non e-enabled
- A range of proactive outgoing customer contacts where Revenue wrote to customers in plain English

- Providing tax and social welfare information to assist them in completing their end of year tax returns
- Providing information to educate customers, for example, explaining when a customer needed to be registered as 'self-assessed' and providing opportunities to de-register where needed.

Looking at comparable periods in previous years, a 60% reduction in contacts was seen, with a burden reduction for those who no longer need to be registered as 'self-assessed'. The pilot was fully adopted, with plans to expand additional services for customers aged 65 and over.

Source: Ireland (2022).

Collaborative services

While many tax administrations develop their own apps internally, Figure 5.3 shows that the vast majority of tax administrations are now creating Application Programming Interfaces (APIs) and that 75% of them are making the APIs available to third party developers. Further, as part of the process of developing APIs, close to 60% of tax administrations are engaging in co-creation with third parties.

APIs are allowing connectivity between systems, people and things without providing direct access, and are the critical enablers of many of the innovative services highlighted in this report. This collaboration is fundamental to the digital transformation of tax administration envisaged in *Tax Administration 3.0* (OECD, 2020[2]).

Figure 5.3. APIs: Development for third party use and co-creation, 2022

Percent of administrations

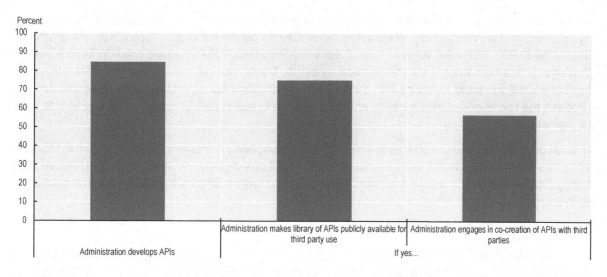

Note: The figure is based on ITTI data from 52 jurisdictions that are covered in this report and that have completed the global survey on digitalisation.
Source: OECD et al. (2022), Inventory of Tax Technology Initiatives, https://www.oecd.org/tax/forum-on-tax-administration/tax-technology-tools-and-digital-solutions/, Table TT7 (accessed on 13 May 2022).

StatLink https://doi.org/10.1787/888934310670

Table 5.3. Interactions for which administrations have published APIs by tax type, 2022

Percent of administrations

Interaction type	Personal income tax	Corporate income tax	Value added tax
Registration for tax	18.2	29.5	29.5
Filing tax returns	43.2	43.2	43.2
Making payments	29.5	31.8	31.8
Requesting extensions of deadlines	11.4	9.1	11.4
Asking for payment arrangements	6.8	4.5	4.5
Making taxpayer confidential enquiries	11.4	20.5	18.2
Filing tax related objections	0.0	2.3	4.5
Dealing with correspondence	25.0	27.3	27.3
Uploading data files onto tax administration's systems	25.0	29.5	31.8
Other interactions *(not by tax type)*		34.1	

Note: The table is based on ITTI data from 52 jurisdictions that are covered in this report and that have completed the global survey on digitalisation.
Source: OECD et al. (2022), Inventory of Tax Technology Initiatives, https://www.oecd.org/tax/forum-on-tax-administration/tax-technology-tools-and-digital-solutions/, Tables TT8, TT9 and TT10 (accessed on 13 May 2022).

The OECD report *Unlocking the digital economy – a guide to unlocking application programming interfaces in government* (OECD, 2019[4]) provides an overview of the practices, techniques and standards used to deliver contemporary and effective digital services for taxpayers through APIs. Box 5.5 highlights some of the ways tax administrations are using them.

Box 5.7. Examples – Using APIs to provide better services

Australia - Enhancing agent services

In 2021, the Australia Taxation Office (ATO) further enhanced their services to agents and third parties by delivering Communication preference and Client communication Application Programming Interfaces (APIs). Providing APIs to Digital Software Providers (DSPs) allows them to build functions that agents can then access via their natural systems. These include communication preference APIs to enable DSPs to build functions into their software that allow tax agents to set preferences for who receives the taxpayer's communication and also retrieve digital copies of communications sent to them or their clients.

In addition, these extended services enable agents to proactively manage their client's communications and drive a further uptake in clients receiving communications digitally. As at the end of December 2021 tax agents had set over 1 million preferences for clients to have their communications delivered digitally to the agent.

Austria – Using APIs for taxpayer services

Incomplete and incorrectly completed tax returns and other submissions cause the tax administration a great deal of effort in correcting errors. The Austrian online tax portal - FinanzOnline - offers services that allow data to be transmitted directly from the accounting systems to the tax administration in a simple way. The data to be transmitted must be mapped in an XML structure, and the transmission takes place via SOAP protocol. The interface is not a one-way street as companies can also request notices and other information from the tax administration and thus use it directly in their own systems.

See Annex 5.A. for links to supporting material.

Greece - Development of APIs for taxpayer services

Timologio is a free application that provides digital issuance of electronic invoices, with more than 120 000 users. All business entities that do not own a computerized accounting system can configure their profile, register their clients, organize their products and services and issue their invoices electronically while sending all necessary information to the myDATA platform at the same time through a fully customizable environment.

This means that business data is standardized, allowing procedures to be simplified which reduces costs for business. The tax administration is also able to prefill fields, and better focus risks. The processes for refunds is also quicker and simpler for compliant businesses.

Hungary - Outline of service-type APIs of the Online Invoice Data Reporting System

The Online Invoice Data Reporting System introduced in Hungary in 2018 a requirement for real-time invoice data-reporting by taxpayers. Therefore, the NTCA also introduced real-time services together with the real-time reporting obligation.

The taxpayer's invoicing program transmits the data report to the tax administration at the time the invoice is closed. Thus, the provision of data does not interfere with the process of issuing invoices and is independent of it. At the same time, the tax administration assesses the invoice data received in real-time and immediately shares the results with taxpayers. Taxpayers can assess the results obtained and decide the appropriate steps for them.

Taxpayers receive these results in their invoicing program, which simplifies their own audit activities. The tax administration therefore does not pre-qualify taxpayers' invoices, allowing them to even make mistakes, but at the same time directs them towards compliant behaviour.

The use of APIs provides not only the possibility of immediate evaluation and feedback, but also easy access to invoice data. For example, a Hungarian company can download supplier invoices from the Online Invoice System via an API to its own accounting program for the processing of invoices which reduces administrative errors.

See Annex 5.A. for links to supporting material.

Peru – New services to support small businesses

The tax administration (SUNAT) has developed specific apps to help SME's and entrepreneurs comply, quickly and easily, with their tax obligations. Through the app '*Emprender SUNAT*', they can check on their tax status, receive messages from SUNAT, generate reports on debts, tax returns and payments as well as obtaining further information on tax benefits. The app also allows SMEs to issues electronic invoices and receipts, and generate reports that can be shared with third parties.

Additionally, 'app Personas SUNAT', allows employed or self-employed individuals to manage their records with SUNAT, including checking on their expense deductions, and filing their annual tax return. The app also allows them to produce tax reports for third parties as well as issuing electronic receipts for any fees.

Sources: Australia (2022), Austria (2022), Greece (2022), Hungary (2022) and Peru (2022).

As the services delivered through APIs become more sophisticated, and play a greater role in delivering a quality service to taxpayers, tax administrations are having to invest more in the management and oversight of their APIs. Box 5.6 sets out some of the work that is being done in this area. At the heart of this work is effective collaboration with third parties to ensure that the systems work smoothly, are accurate and secure and continue to deliver for taxpayers.

Box 5.8. Examples - API management

Canada – API co-creation and management

The Canada Revenue Agency (CRA) provides electronic filing services, through a series of application programming interfaces (APIs), a software system that can send and receive information directly to or from the CRA in real-time. The CRA provides private sector software firms with the necessary tools to create user-friendly and affordable tax-filing solutions that improve service delivery for Canadians, some of which are free. This co-creation model has created a digital ecosystem where a variety of vendors provide tax filings solutions, striving to maximize the ease of their user interface and features provided, and simplifying the tax filing experience for Canadians as a result.

While the CRA relies on the software firms to create user interfaces that facilitate greatly the tax reporting task for Canadians, the CRA also has responsibility for ensuring the products on the market are certified for use and have the ability to interoperate with CRA's filing and processing systems. This rigorous software certification process helps to ensure the quality of the tax information transmitted to the CRA.

During the 2021 filing season, approximately 28 million returns were filed using the CRA's systems, representing close to 91% of all tax returns filed, with the vast majority of those returns processed in near-to-real-time. This public-private collaboration has given the CRA an opportunity to receive feedback from their users, exchange on best practices, and inform prioritization of digital services, while ensuring that Canadians receive the benefits and credits they are entitled to.

See Annex 5.A for links to supporting material.

United Kingdom – Managing software and APIs

HMRC's Making Tax Digital (MTD) Programme is the first phase of the United Kingdom's move towards a modern, digital tax service which is fit for the 21st Century. The MTD programme helps taxpayers reduce common mistakes in their tax returns through the use of software. Such errors cost the Exchequer over GBP 10 billion in lost revenue in 2019-2020.

MTD puts businesses on a path to further digitalisation. By integrating tax management with a range of business processes through software, MTD can help contribute to wider productivity gains for business.

Insight to date demonstrates that MTD is delivering on its core objectives and is working as intended. Independent research indicates that many businesses who are using MTD are experiencing benefits including spending less time on preparing and submitting tax returns, greater accuracy, and improved business operations.

MTD has generated GBP 500 million in Additional Tax Revenue (ATR) since the first phase of mandation in 2019. It is predicted to deliver ATR of around GBP 2.8 billion by 2026–27, as certified by the United Kingdom's Office for Budget Responsibility. This extra revenue is forecast to deliver a reduction in the tax gap caused by error and failure to take reasonable care.

HMRC works closely with the software industry to deliver MTD. The development of MTD compatible software involves building APIs, which enables the software to provide business tax information directly to HMRC.

Sources: Canada (2022) and the United Kingdom (2022).

This collaboration is also opening up possibilities for new service development, often driven by the private sector. Figure 5.4 highlights how common data sharing across government has become, and *Tax Administration 2019* highlighted how tax administrations have become increasingly joined-up with other functions of government to provide better services for citizens (OECD, 2019[5]).

Figure 5.4. Data sharing with other parts of the government, 2022

Percent of administrations

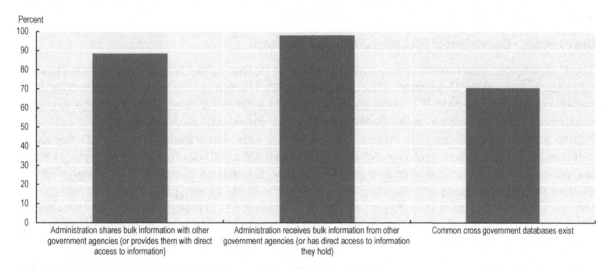

Note: The figure is based on ITTI data from 52 jurisdictions that are covered in this report and that have completed the global survey on digitalisation.
Source: OECD et al. (2022), Inventory of Tax Technology Initiatives, https://www.oecd.org/tax/forum-on-tax-administration/tax-technology-tools-and-digital-solutions/, Table DM3 (accessed on 13 May 2022).

StatLink 📊 https://doi.org/10.1787/888934310689

These efforts to join-up with other government agencies often include a "collect once, use many times" approach. Tax administrations (together with social security agencies) have a special place within government in this respect since they will often hold up-to-date verified information on identity, will be involved in both receiving and making payments and will receive and send information to third parties (such as financial institutions and employers).

Since the last edition of this report tax administrations are reporting that they are deepening their collaboration with an increasing number of organisations outside of government, including in the development of new joined-up services.

Box 5.9. Examples – Developing new collaborative services

Austria – Co creation platform

The co-creation platform of the Austrian tax administration "e3lab – *einfach, elektronisch, effektiv.*" (e3lab – simple, electronically, effective.) was set up in 2017. The participation platform follows the idea of open innovation and gives citizens, business and tax agents the opportunity to engage in the designing, developing and improvement process within the tax administration. This is not restricted to the platform itself but also follows a more holistic approach e.g. through workshops and training groups.

Several projects and services have benefitted from this interaction with taxpayers.

- BMF-APP BMF2go - An app for mobile devices to ease the preparation and submission of tax returns.
- Relaunch of the website / online tax assessment system - FinanzOnline including among others support functions such as guided online assistance, explanatory videos and a chat bot.
- Language manual – Setting up guidelines and examples for a simple and understandable diction without using the typical administrational language.

Currently the platform has around 3 000 members and about 400 ideas have been submitted to the system since the beginning of the challenges.

United States - Department of Education Direct Data Exchange

The United States government coordinates a number of income-based financial assistance programs for students through the Department of Education (ED). After receiving new legislative authority to share certain confidential tax data, IRS collaborated with ED to establish a direct data exchange to support students applying for income-based Federal Student Aid. Previously, students applying for assistance had to authenticate into an IRS system to retrieve this data and transfer it to the ED application themselves. Using this new authority, IRS developed three APIs that will provide the necessary Federal tax information from students and their parent's income tax returns directly to ED to make Federal Student Aid determinations and calculate income-driven loan repayment plans. The APIs use modern technology with a secure system-to-system interface allowing ED to request tax data on-demand and IRS to respond in real-time to millions of such requests annually, while processing large bulk requests overnight.

This new direct data exchange is projected to serve as many as 19 million students by 2024. Together, this legislative and technical solution significantly reduces burden on students applying for financial assistance by eliminating the need for individuals to login to an IRS web portal to request their own income tax data. This allows IRS and ED to operate more efficiently and enhances taxpayer privacy while improving data security and usability.

Sources: Austria (2022) and the United States (2022).

References

OECD (2021), *Behavioural Insights for Better Tax Administration: A Brief Guide*, OECD, Paris, https://www.oecd.org/tax/forum-on-tax-administration/publications-and-products/behavioural-insights-for-better-tax-administration-a-brief-guide.htm (accessed on 13 May 2022). [1]

OECD (2021), *Tax Administration 2021: Comparative Information on OECD and other Advanced and Emerging Economies*, OECD Publishing, Paris, https://doi.org/10.1787/cef472b9-en. [3]

OECD (2020), *Tax Administration 3.0: The Digital Transformation of Tax Administration*, OECD, Paris, https://www.oecd.org/tax/forum-on-tax-administration/publications-and-products/tax-administration-3-0-the-digital-transformation-of-tax-administration.htm (accessed on 13 May 2022). [2]

OECD (2019), *Tax Administration 2019: Comparative Information on OECD and other Advanced and Emerging Economies*, OECD Publishing, Paris, https://doi.org/10.1787/74d162b6-en. [5]

OECD (2019), *Unlocking the Digital Economy - A guide to implementing application programming interfaces in Government*, OECD, Paris, https://www.oecd.org/tax/forum-on-tax-administration/publications-and-products/unlocking-the-digital-economy-guide-to-implementing-application-programming-interfaces-in-government.htm (accessed on 13 May 2022). [4]

Annex 5.A. Links to supporting material (accessed on 13 May 2022)

- Box 5.2. – Chile: Link to the tax administration's website and a video with more details on the taxpayer reports used to promote the accountability of public expenditure:
  - ○ Website: https://www.sii.cl/destacados/reportegt/ (in Spanish); and
  - ○ Video: https://www.youtube.com/watch?v=bDDkLXidstQ (in English).
- Box 5.2. – Hungary: Link to a video regarding the new customer portal: https://www.youtube.com/watch?v=9EOWQNGVIFU
- Box 5.2. – Japan: Link to a presentation with more detail on "Mynaportal": https://www.oecd.org/tax/forum-on-tax-administration/database/b.5.2-japan-mynaportal.pdf
- Box 5.3. – Japan: Link to a presentation on the chatbot: https://www.oecd.org/tax/forum-on-tax-administration/database/b.5.3-japan-chatbot.pdf
- Box 5.5. – Italy: Links to a video and websites with more information on e-invoicing and the app FatturAE:
  - ○ Video on e-invoicing in Italy: https://www.youtube.com/watch?v=pILNi3abCFg
  - ○ E-invoicing website (in Italian): https://www.agenziaentrate.gov.it/portale/web/guest/aree-tematiche/fatturazione-elettronica
  - ○ App FatturAE website (in Italian): https://www.agenziaentrate.gov.it/portale/web/guest/app-fatturae
- Box 5.5. – Malaysia: Link to a flowchart that sets out the myTax service: https://www.oecd.org/tax/forum-on-tax-administration/database/b.5.5-malaysia-mytax-diagram.pdf
- Box 5.7. – Austria: Link to a tax administration's website that contains additional information for software providers on data transmission to the tax administration (in German): https://www.bmf.gv.at/services/finanzonline/informationen-fuer-softwarehersteller.html
- Box 5.7. – Hungary: Link to a video regarding the service-type APIs of the Online Invoice Data Reporting System: https://www.youtube.com/watch?v=8OBQF_NLq6E
- Box 5.8. – Canada: Link to videos with more details on using certified tax software to fill out tax returns:
  - ○ https://www.canada.ca/en/revenue-agency/news/cra-multimedia-library/individuals-video-gallery/learn-taxes-doing-taxes.html
  - ○ https://www.canada.ca/en/revenue-agency/news/cra-multimedia-library/individuals-video-gallery/transcript-filing-online-fast-easy-secure.html

6 Verification and compliance management

Assessing the accuracy and completeness of taxpayer reported information is one of the key functions of tax administrations and critical for supporting voluntary compliance. This chapter takes a closer look at tax administrations' work in this area, including how they manage compliance.

Introduction

The audit, verification and investigation function assesses the accuracy and completeness of taxpayer reported information. This function employs on average thirty percent of tax administration staff and verifies that tax obligations have been met. While this often happens through conducting desk or field based "tax audits", there is an increased use of automated electronic checks, validations and matching of taxpayer information. The undertaking and visibility of these and other compliance actions is critical in supporting voluntary compliance, including through their impacts on perceptions of fairness in the tax system, as well as creating a 'deterrent effect'. This chapter therefore looks at:

- How tax administrations manage compliance risks, including the use of large and integrated data sets;
- The delivery of compliance actions undertaken by tax administrations including moving field audit work into a virtual environment; and
- The work on tax and crime.

Compliance risk management

The OECD report *The Changing Tax Compliance Environment and the Role of Audit* (OECD, 2017[1]) looked at the range of incremental changes occurring across tax administrations which, taken together, were changing the nature of the tax compliance environment, allowing for more targeted and managed compliance.

A significant part of this change is driven by the increased availability of data. As digitalisation proceeds, even more tax related data from taxpayers and third parties is becoming available (for example, data from e-invoicing, online cash registers and financial account information), which is contributing to a clearer understanding of tax gaps. Most tax administrations now apply data sciences techniques and use analytical tools as part of compliance processes (see Table 6.1), and this is explored in more detail later in this chapter. Box 6.1 also contains some examples of the range of data exploration techniques being used by tax administrations.

Another growing trend is the combination of analytics with behavioural analysis to build a more holistic understanding of compliance risks, behavioural patterns and appropriate compliance interventions. Figure 6.1 below, shows the percent of tax administrations who are using behavioural insights in their work.

Figure 6.1. Use of techniques and methodologies to improve compliance, 2020

Percent of administrations that use those techniques and methodologies

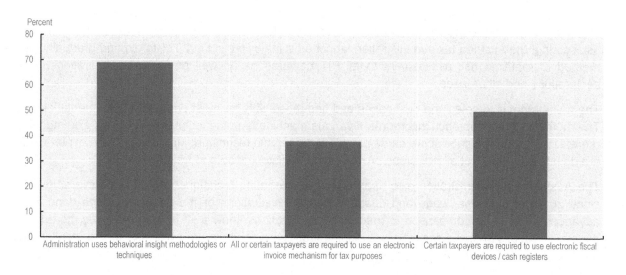

Source: Table A.49 Techniques and methodologies to improve compliance.

StatLink ⧉ https://doi.org/10.1787/888934310708

Box 6.1. Examples - Data exploration

Australia - Financial data matching

The Australian Taxation Office (ATO) has developed a tool that can match up any financial transaction data, regardless of its source or form. It can match, for example:

- Receipts and payments in one group of bank statements to corresponding receipts and payments in another group of bank statements;
- Bank statement receipts/payments to their corresponding entries in accounting records;
- Debit entries in a set of accounting records to their corresponding credit entries within the same accounting records;
- Bank statements or accounting records to pay slips, invoices or inventory records.

This template can process up to 10 000 data items in a single tranche, and operates approximately 30x faster than a human analyst and has better than human accuracy on most metrics. The robust fuzzy matching engine is undeterred by abbreviations or typographical errors in the data, and automatically detects and reconciles compound payments (that is, a single entry in one data source that matches to a number of smaller entries in another data source). The template also outputs match confidence indicators, and produce exceptions report (e.g. unmatched items) automatically.

Investigators and auditors use this template to confirm the details of suspicious transactions by corroborating them within or across different data sets and identifying relationships that are not apparent to the human eye.

Austria - Digital innovations as regards electronic compliance checks and real-time audits

In 2020, the Austrian tax administration has deployed a real-time risk assessment for PIT declarations for employed individuals. Based on this scoring, cases are selected for desk audits. An evaluation of the year 2020 revealed a doubling in the hit-rate (cases identified as having a supplemental claim) while the number of cases selected decreased by more than 40%. Due to the success of the innovation in risk scoring, the Austrian tax administration launched a major project in 2021 to expand gradually this method of real-time risk assessment to all PIT declarations as well as to VAT declarations, CIT declarations and other taxes.

The main target is to select the best cases and find those with the most probable supplemental claim. The methodological approach incorporates various machine learning techniques such as tree models, regression models, balance score cards as well as ensemble techniques. In addition, also expert rules are developed, since not all risk areas provide enough historical data to train models.

The Austrian tax administration also uses supervised learning techniques for central case selection since 2016 for business, wage and customs audits. Evaluations of the case selections done with advanced analytics in comparison to manual case selections show a lift in the hit-rate by more than double, i.e. audits of cases selected by machine learning algorithms are twice as likely to result in an audit surplus of more than EUR 10 000.

Canada - Digital Forensic Investigation Tools

The Canada Revenue Agency (CRA) engages in complex investigations where large volumes of data are gathered pursuant to search warrants or other means. The CRA utilises various digital forensic tools that assist the user in narrowing down what may be relevant to an investigation thus saving substantial time and costs on an investigation, including the following:

- Advanced tools that learn as the investigators are reviewing and identifying relevant data and evidence thereby allowing investigators to save time in finding documents relevant to an investigation.
- Tools that enable users to view visual linkages, clusters and patterns which help investigators focus on key areas of potential interest.
- Tools that identify and extract key patterns within evidence which may be relevant to the investigation such as telephone numbers, credit card numbers, social insurance numbers, etc.
- Tools that perform searches of contents of data along with the metadata associated with the file, as well as "fuzzy" searches that enable a search of text that is close to what the investigator may be looking for.
- Tools that create dictionaries from seized data that are used to form passwords for brute force attacks on encrypted or password protected documents.

For business intelligence analysts, the use of electronic discovery software provides structure to a high volume of unstructured data. It also focuses efforts on the most relevant information so criminal investigations can act swiftly. The software also permits collaboration from various workplaces. In the current environment, access from different worksites is essential.

Canada - Refining services through analysis

The CRA faces unique analytics problems, and has developed and empirically tested new methods to address these gaps. Scatterplot matrices are useful for exploring low-dimensional datasets (i.e., datasets with only a few columns). However, currently there are no ideal alternatives when dealing with high-dimensional data (i.e., datasets with many columns). The work in question presents a data exploration method that is easily applicable in high-dimensional contexts, and is designed to yield similar analytical information to scatterplot matrices. This is done by combining complimentary information from (a) an overall multivariate model and (b) a series of bivariate models.

As an example, this may be applied when mining call centre databases, wherein callers' requests are logged and tracked as they are filled. Such a database may have thousands of variables to investigate. These models developed by the CRA, permit analysts to sift efficiently through these databases to find information that can refine business practices or inform decision-making. In order to ensure this approach provides accurate insights, we have tested it rigorously via a series of simulation studies. In these contexts, the Agency commonly uses these methods to look at which factors relate to the time it takes to complete external requests. This information is then used to spot bottlenecks, oddities, or inefficiencies.

Italy – Using data to estimate the VAT Gap

The Bottom-Up Tax Gap Estimation initiative is a new methodology for the estimation of the VAT gap based on the use of information from the tax assessment database. The estimates are obtained by combining traditional methods, modern machine learning techniques and 'nearest neighbor' procedures.

This "machine learning assisted" methodology produces a final outcome of a set of individual values that can be used to obtain estimates of the VAT gap at different levels of detail. This work will support tax administration by providing clear focus for compliance activity, and data for policy making. It also allows the gap to be examined by different taxpayer behaviours.

See Annex 6.A for supporting material.

Sources: Australia (2022), Austria (2022), Canada (2022) and Italy (2022).

Increasing availability of data

As more and more data is stored electronically, and the transfer, storage and integration of data has become easier through the application of new techniques and processes, there has been a huge increase in the amount of data available to tax administrations for compliance purposes. New data sources include:

- **Data from devices**: Data can be collected from devices that register transactions such as online cash registers and trip computers for taxis and trucks, and also gate registrations from barriers and weigh bridges.

- **Data from banks, merchants or payment intermediaries and service providers**: This allows direct verification of income or assets reported by the taxpayer. Some jurisdictions already receive transaction details or transaction totals for taxpayers on a regular basis.

- **Data from suppliers**: Collecting data from suppliers, either directly or through the taxpayer, allows a more complete picture to be drawn about the activities and income of the taxpayer. This is seen in the increasing use of e-invoicing systems which, as noted in Chapter 4, allows some tax administrations to prefill tax returns.

- **Data from the customer**: This is easiest in cases where the number of customers is limited and known, but increasingly mechanisms to leverage customers in compliance are being used, for example in the verification of cash receipts.

- **Unstructured data concerning the taxpayer**: Increasingly electronic traces relevant to business activities and transactions can be found on the internet and in social media. Also the analysis of unstructured data can improve response times and accuracy as set out in the example from Australia in Box 6.1.

- *Data from other government agencies*: Data held by other government agencies for example for licencing, regulatory or social security purposes can be relevant in verifying tax returns or in risk assessments. For example, the French tax administration uses information from local property maps, municipalities, the real estate registry and aerial photographs available on the web to identify real estate that, due to its use and value, is subject to special tax (see Box 6.2).
- *Data from international partners*: New international exchanges of data commencing under the Common Reporting Standard and Country-by-Country Reporting is massively increasing the quantity of data available on international activity and providing useful information for audit and case selection processes and in some cases for prefilling of tax returns.

Box 6.2. Examples - Increased availability of data

Argentina - Simple and Pro-Forma VAT Tax Return

A Digital VAT Ledger is compulsory for all taxpayers liable for VAT in Argentina (around a million taxpayers), and for a defined group of VAT exempt taxpayers (even though they are not required to file VAT tax returns). During a first phase of implementation, around 20 000 taxpayers - who issued a small amount of electronic invoices and had a single activity of professional services - were selected for a new simplified procedure which comprised two parts:

- A Simplified Digital VAT Ledger: This shows the taxpayers all the electronic invoices they issued and received, and taxpayers must confirm or correct the record for that particular period. When invoices are missing, they can be added to the app manually and invoices not related to the commercial activity must be deleted (e.g., personal expenses).
- A Simplified VAT tax return: Based on the data of the Digital VAT Ledger, a Value Added Tax return is automatically generated and the amount due is assessed. The amounts cannot be edited. If necessary, the Digital VAT Ledger has to be modified.

As a next stage, a new digital VAT return will be gradually implemented. This return will be prefilled with all the amounts entered in the Digital VAT Ledger (sales, purchases, exports, tax debits and credits, etc.). In the future, this pro-forma return will be compulsory for all VAT liable taxpayers. Through this work there should be increased compliance, more reliable data, reduced business burdens and reduced fraud opportunities.

See Annex 6.A for supporting material.

Canada - Follow the Dollar Research Initiative

The CRA has developed its ability to integrate data from various assessment and compliance activities related to PIT, CIT, and VAT (GST/HST) tax programmes, creating a holistic understanding of effectiveness of different interventions and enabling outcomes to be quantified.

The Follow the Dollar project provides a view of the life cycle of tax returns, from initial assessment to resolution, with associated analysis. As a result of the initiative, CRA can identify trends, track the impact of interventions, policy changes, and more. This initiative allows CRA to follow the dollar in our processing from end-to-end. Beginning with the initial filing of a tax return by the taxpayer/registrant or entity, we are able to monitor the dollar through activities performed to enhance compliance, then follow it through appeals (if warranted) and finally through to payment, refund, collection or write-off, measuring outcomes along the way. In so doing, CRA is able to calculate certain metrics, such as audit yield. Additionally, this initiative is enabling further research such as exploring the write-off predictability rate for the Agency, as well as identifying clusters, trends and compliance gaps.

France - Innovative Land Tenure

To improve the process of detecting undeclared constructions or developments, the French tax administration (DGFiP) uses artificial intelligence and data enhancement based on aerial photographs taken by the *Institut national de l'information géographique et forestière* (IGN) as part of the "Foncier innovant" project.

The algorithms will make it possible to extract the outlines of buildings and swimming pools from the public aerial images of the IGN, which can be consulted by everyone on the website www.geoportail.gouv.fr. A computer process then verifies, from the declarations made by the owners to the tax authorities, whether the elements thus detected on the images are correctly taxed for direct local taxes (property tax in particular). An agent of the tax authorities then systematically verifies each anomaly detected before any operation of reminding the owner of the property and ultimately of taxation.

See Annex 6.A for supporting material.

Lithuania - Increasing transparency of 2nd hand car transactions

According to the data of the Lithuanian State Tax Inspectorate (STI), used car trade, repair and car part trade sectors are classified as one of the highest risk sectors for tax evasion. Based on the results of the study concluded in 2018, the VAT gap within the sector for trade of used care was more than EUR 38 million. Therefore, STI is especially keen on performing monitoring and control activities within this sector.

In order to resolve the problem of unscrupulous salespersons operating within the used car trade sector, a new accounting framework for vehicle owners has been developed with changes in the legislation requiring all cars present within the country to bear a unique vehicle owner declaration code (SDK). The code allows a specific car to be traced back to its owner within Lithuania.

Prior to the entry of the vehicle into Lithuania, the owner of vehicle is required to have a valid SDK. The registration and sale of vehicle is not allowed without SDK and it is required to be published in all vehicle advertisements. By checking more than 6 000 vehicles on roads and parking lots and more than 22 000 vehicle advertisements on the internet, almost 21 000 total cases of missing SDK and/or failure to publicly disclose the SDK were uncovered. The offenders received warnings and their information has been logged for repeat investigations following the end of the grace period.

The newly implemented system has resulted in a positive impact being realised within a couple months after launch. It has highlighted 22 persons possibly engaged in the operation of unregistered car trade, EUR 109 000 of undeclared income have been disclosed, and six persons have registered their car trading operations. This is helping create a fair market while car salespersons causing the highest risk are being identified and purchasers can check the sale is trustworthy.

See Annex 6.A for supporting material.

Spain – Analysing feedback from verification actions

The Spanish Tax Agency's Strategic Plan 2020-2023 includes plans for prevention and control of tax and customs fraud, and includes a complete analysis of the results of compliance actions, in order to ensure that tax regularizations become an additional tool for obtaining improvements in voluntary compliance by taxpayers. In this regard, it is important to highlight the importance of the feedback from the verification actions, consisting of gathering information on the reasons that lead to the regularisation of the taxpayers included in the control plans.

This information is incorporated into the Tax Agency's databases and allows for the qualitative evaluation of the verification actions. This helps in the planning of future actions, which will be oriented towards the programmes, profiles or risks that are of most help in reducing the most significant non-compliance. The collection of this information is obtained through predefined forms, in which the officials select the main reason or reasons for the tax regularisation and quantify it. This is done within a standardized table of reasons for regularisation, weighting the reason for regularisation against the amount of the tax assessment.

The analysis of the reasons for regularisation is carried out through computer tools that can support massive data processing. This allows structured information to be obtained on the specific risk areas of the main taxes of the Spanish tax system as well as knowledge of the reasons that lead to the regularisation.

See Annex 6.A for supporting material.

Sources: Argentina (2022), Canada (2022), France (2022), Lithuania (2022) and Spain (2022).

There are, though, some emerging risks to the availability of large data sets. In particular, it is increasingly possible for data relevant to the tax administration in one jurisdiction to be held within the territory of another jurisdiction. In these circumstances, it can be difficult to obtain the data on an automatic basis from the data holder located in another jurisdiction. This could make it more difficult to risk assess in some circumstances, as well as making it more difficult to prefill tax returns and to further develop compliance-by-design processes.

An example of this comes from the growth of the sharing and gig economy facilitated through online platforms which can operate across border. This may become an increasing risk as the online economy grows, particularly if it is accompanied by a shift from salaried employment (and the reporting of incomes by employers) to self-employment. This issue was considered in the OECD report *The Sharing and Gig Economy: Effective Taxation of Platform Sellers* (OECD, 2019[2]). That report looked at a number of strategies currently being adopted by tax administrations as well as their limitations and recommended the development of standardised reporting requirements to facilitate possible future automatic exchange of information between tax administrations. It also led to the development of:

- A set of Model Rules that when used in legislation require digital platforms to collect information on the income realised by those offering accommodation, transport and personal services through platforms and to report the information to tax authorities (OECD, 2020[3]).
- A Code of Conduct to facilitate a possible standard approach to co-operation between administrations and platforms on providing information and support to platform sellers on their tax obligations while minimising compliance burdens (OECD, 2020[4]).

Another risk that has been identified is that posed by digital financial assets (DFAs), such as cryptocurrencies. The owners of DFAs can be very difficult to trace even though they may be linked to the creation of a specific digital wallet (which is somewhat similar to a bank account). Tracking down the individuals or entities behind particular wallet addresses is at best very difficult and resource intensive.

While not a risk as such, it should also be noted that data protection requirements could limit the circumstances in which data can be kept, processed or shared. This is a key consideration for administrations in designing systems which rely on large data sets and the retention of data.

Sharpened targeting of risks

Data science

Over recent years, the application of advanced analytics to risk management and risk targeting is becoming increasingly common;

- Figure 6.2 shows 80% of tax administrations reporting using big data in their work, and of those that use big data nearly all are using it to improve their compliance work.
- Of the 58 tax administrations covered by this report, 52 report using data science / analytical tools with the remaining administrations in the process of preparing the use of such tools going forward (see Table A.51).
- Similarly, the use of artificial intelligence, including machine learning, for risk assessments and detecting fraud is already undertaken or in the process of being implemented by the majority of administrations covered in this publication (see Table 6.1 and Figure 6.3).

This increasingly sophisticated use of analytics on expanded data sets is leading to a sharpening of risk management and the development of a range of intervention actions, including through automated processes. A selection of examples is included in Box 6.3. Additionally, the OECD report *Advanced Analytics for Tax Administration: Putting data to work* (OECD, 2016[5]) provides practical guidance on how tax administrations can use analytics to support compliance and service delivery.

Table 6.1. Application of data science, 2020

Percent of administrations

Status of implementation and use	Data science / analytical tools			Artificial intelligence, including machine learning			Robotic process automation		
	2018	2020	Difference in percentage points (p.p.)	2018	2020	Difference in p.p.	2018	2020	Difference in p.p.
Technology implemented and used	73.7	89.5	+15.8	31.6	47.4	+15.8	22.8	40.3	+17.5
Technology in the implementation phase for future use	17.5	10.5	-7.0	15.8	29.8	+14.0	14.0	12.3	-1.7
Technology not used, incl. situations where implementation has not started	8.8	0.0	-8.8	52.6	22.8	-29.8	63.2	47.4	-15.8

Source: Tables A.51 Innovative technologies: Implementation and usage (Part 1) and A.52 Innovative technologies: Implementation and usage (Part 2).

Figure 6.2. Use of big data for analytical purposes, 2022

Percent of administrations

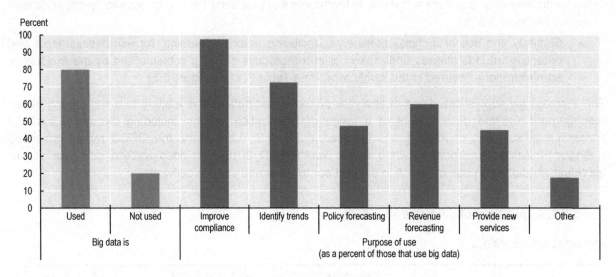

Note: The figure is based on ITTI data from 52 jurisdictions that are covered in this report and that have completed the global survey on digitalisation.
Source: OECD et al. (2022), Inventory of Tax Technology Initiatives, https://www.oecd.org/tax/forum-on-tax-administration/tax-technology-tools-and-digital-solutions/, Table DM3 (accessed on 13 May 2022).

StatLink 🔗 https://doi.org/10.1787/888934310727

Figure 6.3. Use of artificial intelligence, 2022

Percent of administrations

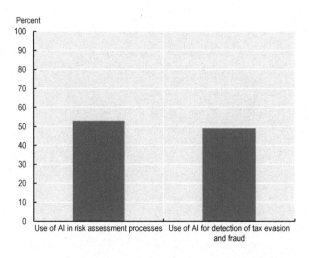

Note: The figure is based on ITTI data from 52 jurisdictions that are covered in this report and that have completed the global survey on digitalisation.
Source: OECD et al. (2022), Inventory of Tax Technology Initiatives, https://www.oecd.org/tax/forum-on-tax-administration/tax-technology-tools-and-digital-solutions/, Table DM3 (accessed on 13 May 2022).

StatLink 🔗 https://doi.org/10.1787/888934310746

Box 6.3. Examples - Using analytics to sharpen the targeting of risks

Australia - Electronic compliance checks and real-time audits

The ATO are trialling a new feature for taxpayers as part of the lodgement process for income tax returns to help them comply with their tax obligations. The intent of this new feature is to increase positive voluntary compliance for small businesses by addressing risks at time of lodgement using real time analytics and nudge messaging. If there is an anomaly based on industry benchmarks, the system will pop up with a message that prompts the client to double check their figures before submitting their income tax return. When a business is operating significantly outside the key benchmark range for their industry, this does not automatically mean they have done anything wrong, however it does indicate something is unusual and may prompt us to contact them for further information in the future. An example nudge message might be "Your cost of sales amount of <xx> and total expenses amount of <xx> are higher than the small business benchmarks for your circumstances. Please review these amounts and the income that has been reported."

At present this feature is only available to individuals running a business, however, even with this limited trial the ATO have seen about 25% of clients who have received a nudge message go back and make an adjustment to their income tax return before they finalise the lodgement. This has resulted in savings to the taxpayer and the ATO through the prevention of subsequent compliance activity.

Bulgaria – Using machine learning to identify missing traders

To combat VAT fraudulent transactions the Bulgarian National Revenue Agency (BNRA) for over ten years has been using a two-step process. First, BNRA computes a rules-based system risk score for the universe of the VAT-registered taxpayers in the country. Following this, the top-ranked taxpayers are further analysed with the view of establishing if each of them is a part of a missing trader chain. This two-stage process therefore discretely combines data analytics with operational knowledge. As such it is highly labour-intensive as requires input from the most experienced BNRA tax professionals. In 2019 a co-operation was established between the BNRA and the Tax Administration Research Centre (University of Exeter Business School), and University College London. The main objective of this co-operation was to develop a scalable predictive model, which automatically identifies missing traders. A key aspect of the methodological approach developed is that the network structure of all VAT transactions (through sales/purchases invoices) provides important information which can (and should) be used to identify abnormal VAT transactions through the production chain.

In early 2021, BNRA started implementing the predictive model, partially utilising the information structure emerging from the rich VAT transactions data collected. The first results have shown that such an approach can achieve both faster identification of fraudulent VAT transactions, but also a significantly higher proportion of identified real missing traders. This means the time a missing trader begins its fraudulent activities and the time it is identified by BNRA is on average reduced by 15%. Importantly, the predictive model can now identify fraudulent transactions without relying solely on the established risk rules used in risk assessment, thereby making identification more flexible.

Chile – Detecting VAT non compliance

Chilean tax legislation allows for the VAT on specific expenses borne by taxpayers to be used as credits against VAT and other special taxes (in addition to input VAT). However, Chile does not have information that confirms these expenses, creating opportunities for fraud. As a result, a mathematical model has been generated to estimate the probability that such "special credits" are fraudulent, which together with the business analysis, allows for improved risk analysis. Some taxpayers also declare VAT credits for purchases that are not related to their business activity; usually personal expenses.

Chile is therefore using models to analyse electronic invoices and estimate whether these purchases are from business activity.

In addition, six analytical monitoring dashboards have been prepared covering: VAT; Special VAT Credits; Issuance of Electronic Invoices; Income and Expenses; Electronic Fee Tickets; and Financial Ratios for Large Taxpayers. Each dashboard has a series of filters, which allow the analyst to explore different segments of taxpayers, and detect abnormal behaviour, trends, patterns, etc. This is also used to prioritise taxpayer segments for analysis, allowing a more efficient use of resources.

China (People's Republic of) – Selecting cases for e-audit

With the rapid development of cloud computing, machine learning, data mining and other technologies, the *'Audit big data case selection and case study and judgment system'* developed by the State Tax Administration (STA) makes full use of big data for data modelling to accurately explore various high-risk cases, and identify the key targets of tax audit.

There are two main advantages of the system:

- It is supported by various national tax data sources collected by the STA as well as by visualization technology to showcase taxpayers' tax related behaviours in multiple dimensions. Users can intuitively identify the risk characteristics of taxpayers and flag their illegal behaviours;
- The process of case source selection is integrated with advanced machine learning and data mining algorithms to improve the efficiency of data analysis, increasing the accuracy of risk assessment.

Since the launch of the system, this work has in particular played an important role in the two-year project to tackle false VAT invoices and export VAT refund fraud, compliance in the cultural and entertainment industry and the investigation of major cases.

Georgia - System of data processing and analysis

The creation of data processing and analysis system is part of a wider data warehouse development project that was completed in 2021. The ultimate and main goal of the program is to collect and sort data available from the Revenue Service database and other third-party data sources and use them to strengthen the analytical capabilities of the Revenue Service.

As part of the creation of a system for data processing and analysis, the data processing and analysis system infrastructure were optimized. Different types of standard reports have been created in the data processing and analysis system, which are updated on a daily basis. Tax risk modules have been implemented and automated, which allows a systematic assessment of the tax risk of taxpayers and tax returns, using specific logic and indicators.

The programme has already reduced the time required to process specific information, as well as the risk of human error related to information retrieval and processing. It has also allowed prompt monitoring of important ongoing projects (such as the automatic VAT refund process), and the continuous receipt and processing of information from third parties. Furthermore it is being used for the operational assessment, ranking and preparation of specific tax risks (e.g. undeclared inventories).

Sources: Australia (2022), Bulgaria (2022), Chile (2022), China (People's Republic of) (2022) and Georgia (2022).

Taxpayer programmes

Another approach for targeted risk management is the creation of units looking into the tax affairs of specific taxpayer segments. Two specific areas where tax administrations have found it advantageous to manage specific groups of taxpayers on a segmented basis are large business taxpayers, and high net wealth individuals (HNWIs). The rationale for focusing administration resources on managing these groups revolves around the:

- **Significance of tax compliance risks**: due to the nature and type of transactions, offshore activities, opportunity and strategies to minimise tax liabilities; and in the case of large business, the differences between financial accounting profits and the profits computed for tax purposes.
- **Complexity of business and tax dealings**: particularly the breadth of their business interests and in the case of HNWI, the mix of private and tax affairs.
- **Integrity of the tax system**: the importance of being able to assure stakeholders about the work undertaken with these high profile groups of taxpayers.

Additionally, in the case of large taxpayers, a small number of taxpayers are typically responsible for a disproportionate share of tax revenue collected. Data collected as part of the 2021 International Survey on Revenue Administration (ISORA) indicates that for most jurisdictions between 30% and 60% of their total net revenue, including withholding payments on behalf of employees, was received from taxpayers covered by their large taxpayer programmes (see Figure 6.4). On average, 2.3% of corporate taxpayers covered by those programmes account for 43% of all revenue collected (see Table 6.2).

Table 6.2. Importance of large taxpayer offices / programmes (LTO/P), 2020

FTEs in LTO/P as percentage of total FTEs	Corporate taxpayers managed through LTO/P as percentage of active corporate taxpayers	Percentage of net revenue administered under LTO/P in relation to total net revenue collected by the tax administration	FTEs on audit, investigation and other verification function in the LTO/P as percentage of total FTEs in LTO/P	Total value of additional assessments raised through LTO/P as percentage of total value of additional assessments raised from audits
4.1	2.3	42.8	66.6	28.7

Note: The table shows the average percentages across the jurisdictions that were able to provide the information.
Source: Table D.9 Segmentation ratios: LTO/Ps.

While the management of these groups of taxpayers is often undertaken as a programme, in a large number of jurisdictions these programmes are also structural involving a Large Taxpayer Office or HNWI unit. The scope of the work of these units varies considerably, ranging from undertaking traditional audit activity, through to "full service" approaches (see Figure 6.5). However, on average two-thirds of tax administration staff in large taxpayer offices or programmes are working on audit, investigation and other verification related issues (see Table 6.2).

Figure 6.4. Percentage of revenue administered through large taxpayer offices/programmes, 2020

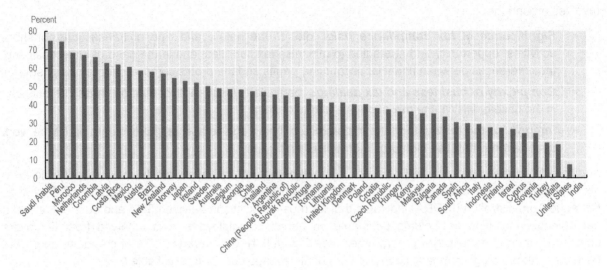

Source: Table D.9 Segmentation ratios: LTO/Ps

StatLink ᴴᴵˢᴸ https://doi.org/10.1787/888934310765

Figure 6.5. Large taxpayer offices / programmes: Existence and functions carried out, 2020

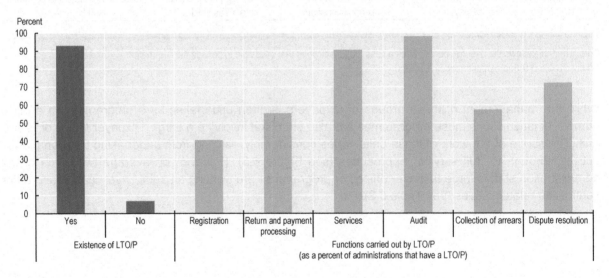

Source: Table A.15 Large taxpayer office / program: Existence and functions

StatLink ᴴᴵˢᴸ https://doi.org/10.1787/888934310784

Figure 6.6. HNWI programmes, 2020

Percent of administrations

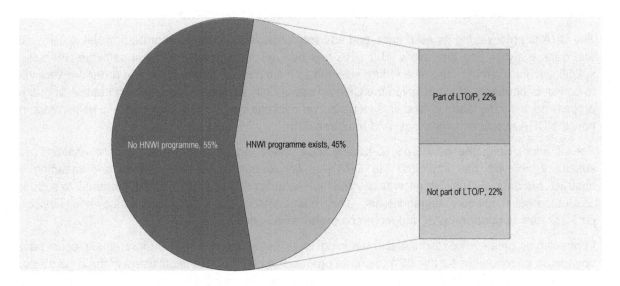

Source: Table A.18 High net wealth individuals (HNWIs) program.

StatLink ᵐˢ⁣ https://doi.org/10.1787/888934310803

Planning for future risks

While it is key for tax administrations to understand current compliance risks and prepare appropriate response strategies, it is equally important to understand and prevent risks which may arise in the future. The increasing availability of data along with the enhanced capacity of tax administrations to handle and analyse that data allows tax administrations to more robustly assess future tax risks. Figure 6.2 highlights the large number of tax administrations who engage in forecasting, which is putting them in a position to assess where new compliance risks may arise and develop in time the necessary mitigation strategies.

This is particularly important as jurisdictions emerge from the COVID-19 pandemic. Tax administrations report that the pandemic influenced taxpayer's compliance behaviour as government lockdowns and related measures affected the income streams of many taxpayers, resulting in reduced profits or even losses. As most administrations reduced or suspended compliance activities, this also impacted the data available to accurately assess risk. The sophisticated modelling analytics and modelling skills that tax administrations built up before the pandemic have been used to respond to these challenges, and to take account of any changes in taxpayer behaviour.

An interesting development within tax administrations is the recognition that the power of data analysis needs to be decentralised and spread more widely across the organisation. Through this tax administrations can be ready to identify emerging risks more quickly, and identify possible early interventions. As a result, tax administrations are now also exploring how artificial intelligence can be embedded into compliance processes across the organisation, and it is likely that this will be central to the digital transformation of compliance management, and risk management in the future. Examples of this can be seen in Box 6.4 below.

Box 6.4. Examples - Embedding AI across the organisation

Canada - Advanced Data Analysis Techniques For Assurance Engagements

The CRA is empowering its assurance and advisory professionals to incorporate artificial intelligence and data analytics into their work. The CRA has evolved from using traditional software, marketed specifically for internal auditors, and has invested in learning how to use tools that are more versatile to power its analytics. This has given the CRA an opportunity to use the many robust natural language processing, machine learning, and data visualization packages available in these tools to help transform how the CRA accesses, processes, and analyzes data.

For instance, using the new tools to deploy topic modelling, abstractive text summarization, and sentiment analysis has improved the CRA's ability to quickly identify themes and meaning in unstructured data, such as interview notes and high volumes of web articles and documents, to support assurance and advisory engagements. This has enabled the CRA's assurance and advisory professionals to perform faster and more comprehensive reviews.

Furthermore, data visualization and interfacing tools using open source programming code have opened up opportunities for the CRA to create products to help non-technical users in the organization incorporate structured data into their reports more easily. One such example is a technique that the CRA has developed to help show interconnections between corporate risks in a visually appealing manner to promote further analysis and clearer reporting.

Singapore – Developing an AI strategy

The Inland Revenue Authority of Singapore (IRAS) is scaling up the use of data and AI across all functions, including through the development of new AI solutions and Minimum Viable Products (MVP) to better manage tax non-compliance and improve service delivery. IRAS' AI initiatives include:

- Anomaly Detection – Traditionally, case selection models under Corporate Income Tax were built based on supervised learning and therefore could only detect known patterns by learning from the past. To uncover unknown risks and to complement existing models, IRAS adopted anomaly detection techniques and developed an MVP to detect anomalies in Corporate Income Tax Returns for officers' review. The MVP has successfully identified several anomalous cases which could potentially result in notable tax recoveries.

- Intelligent Network Analysis Tool – IRAS employed graph database as a solution to address challenges faced by auditors when analysing complex layers of relationships and networks. Instead of relying on commercial tools, IRAS implemented an in-house network visualizer with graph database as the underlying technology to address the auditors' needs. This new tool provides auditors with customised functionalities to analyse intricate, multi-layered relationships between entities during audits/investigations. It can also uncover relationships more than 10 connections deep in a real-time manner.

- Service Quality Monitoring – IRAS has developed Natural Language Processing models to rate 100% of live chats for service quality monitoring. The new AI solution can boost objectivity and productivity of service quality monitoring, enabling IRAS to identify chats that require attention and take proactive actions to improve the service experience.

Sources: Canada (2022) and Singapore (2022).

Delivery of compliance actions

The type of "compliance actions" undertaken by tax administrations to determine whether taxpayers have properly reported their tax liability is changing. As set out earlier, the increasing availability of data and the introduction of sophisticated analytical models are allowing administrations to better identify returns, claims or transactions which might require further review or be fraudulent. Furthermore, these models, many of which can operate in real-time, are allowing administrations to conduct automated electronic checks on all returns or on transactions of a particular type.

Electronic compliance checks

While traditional audits (including comprehensive, issue or desk audits) are often the primary verification activities, the use of automated electronic checks or using rules-based approaches to treat some defined risks (e.g. automatically denying a claim, issuing a letter or matching a transaction) is providing administrations with more effective and efficient ways to undertake some of this work. Box 6.5 sets out examples of this.

These approaches do, however, raise the question of how to reflect those automated electronic checks in the performance information that administrations report in ISORA data. To include all checking may distort coverage, adjustment and yield rates. However where it replaces previously undertaken manual actions it would seem appropriate to reflect what administrations are now doing in this area.

In this respect, the 2021 version of the ISORA survey invited participants to break down the total value of additional assessments raised from audit and verification actions into (i) audits and (ii) electronic compliance checks (defined as electronic checks, validation and matching of taxpayer information).

Only a few administrations were able to provide information on electronic compliance checks. However, for some of those administrations electronic compliance checks make-up an important part of the additional assessments raised through all audits and verification actions. (See Table A.34)

> ### Box 6.5. Brazil - Electronic compliance checks
>
> **Brazil - High Performance Inspection work processes**
>
> The Internal Revenue Service of Brazil (RFB) uses an internal development platform, which brings together a set of tools for data crossing, data mining, graph analytics and application of some AI techniques. This platform also uses a big data environment to perform queries on large tables, with volumes in the order of petabytes. For example, the electronic invoice table totals trillions of records and hundreds of pieces of information about each one. In addition to ready-to-use tools, the development platform allows tax administration members to build their own tools or improve existing ones. It can be accomplished by writing new scripts, shared in a collaborative space, and cataloged to be used as automation assets. For those who are not proficient in programming languages, they can use a 'no-code' programming style created on the platform under the name of 'Visual Script'. This platform facilitated a strategy called 'High Performance Inspection' (FAPE) where tax intelligence was combined with the Big Data environment. This meant multiple regional teams could collaborate and perform cross-reference on different databases, including digital tax bookkeeping, digital accounting, electronic invoices, financial movement data, registration data, among others. FAPE also included the automatic generation of letters to taxpayers in self-assessment where there are divergences on the declared values from the data held. The high level of automation optimizes the use of the workforce, making it possible to dramatically increase the fiscal presence of the small regional teams.
>
> In recent years, an increasing numbers of taxpayers have been summoned by means of these automatic notifications. In 2021, there were more than 40 000 taxpayers summoned, totaling BRL 7.4 billion in amounts subject to self-assessment, which would not have been possible without the automation provided by the FAPE work.
>
> Sources: Brazil (2022).

Audits

While previous ISORA surveys distinguished between audit adjustment rates by audit type, this has changed with the introduction of the 2020 ISORA survey. Since then administrations are invited to provide information for all audits combined. A data comparison is therefore only possible for the years 2018 to 2020.

Table 6.3. Audit adjustment rates and additional assessments raised

	2018	2019	2020
Audit adjustment rates – in percent (41 jurisdictions)	55.6	56.5	55.9
Additional assessments raised through audits as a percentage of tax collections (48 jurisdictions)	4.2	4.2	4.5

Note: The table shows the average audit adjustment rates and additional assessments raised through audits (excluding electronic compliance checks) for those jurisdictions that were able to provide the information for the years 2018, 2019 and 2020. Data for India has been excluded from the calculations for additional assessments raised as it would distort the average ratios. The number of jurisdictions for which data was available is shown in parenthesis.
Source: Table D.22 Audits: Hit rate and additional assessments raised.

Looking at the data, there are some general observations that can be made:

- On average, **audit adjustment rates** have remained stable over the period 2018 to 2020 (see Table 6.3). However, the rates vary significantly across the administrations covered by this report ranging from as low as 10% in Slovenia and Norway to as high as 95% and more in Brazil, Bulgaria and Morocco (see Figure 6.7.). (High adjustment rates can of course result from highly targeted audits.)

- The importance of audits can also be seen when looking at the **additional assessments raised**. On average, the additional assessments raised from audits correspond to around 4.5% of total revenue collections. This has been relatively flat over the years 2018, 2019 and 2020 (see Table 6.3). Looking at the jurisdiction level data, it can be seen that there are significant differences across the 51 administrations that were able to provide data for 2020 (see Figure 6.8).

- Breaking this down by tax type, it shows that the ratio of additional assessments raised to tax collected is the greatest for corporate income tax (CIT). On average, CIT additional assessment raised as a percentage of CIT collected is 11.7%, more than double the percentage for value added tax (4.6%) and more than four times the percentage for personal income tax (2.5%) (see Figure 6.9).

- In many jurisdictions, the **additional assessments raised through large taxpayer offices or programmes** (LTO/P) make-up a significant share of the total additional assessments raised from audits (see Figure 6.10). On average, LTO/Ps contribute around 30% of the total additional assessments raised from audits (see Table 6.2).

Figure 6.7. Audit adjustment rates, 2020

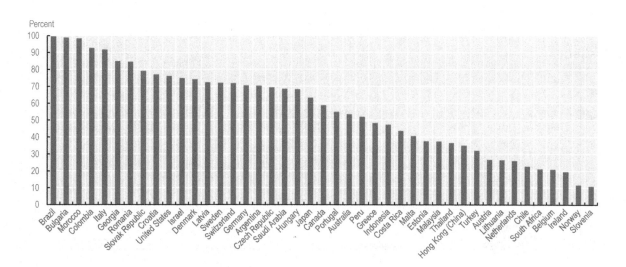

Source: Table D.22 Audits: Hit rate and additional assessments raised.

StatLink ᵐˢ▄ https://doi.org/10.1787/888934310822

Figure 6.8. Additional assessments raised through audit as percentage of tax collections, 2020

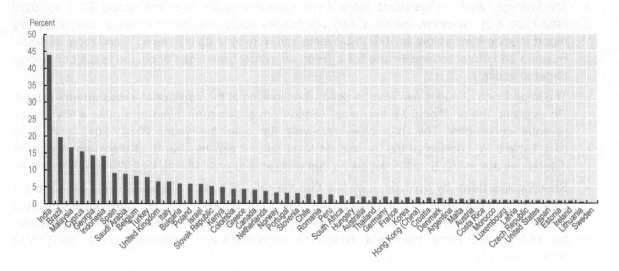

Source: Table D.22 Audits: Hit rate and additional assessments raised.

StatLink https://doi.org/10.1787/888934310841

Figure 6.9. Additional assessments raised through audit as percentage of tax collected by tax type, 2020

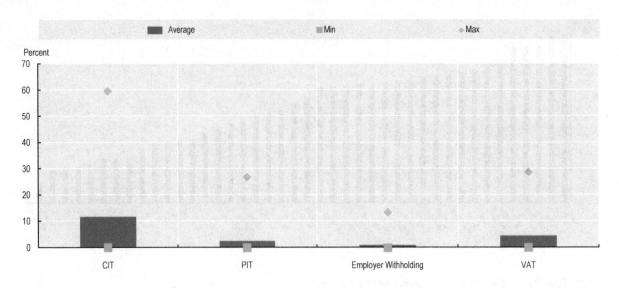

Source: D.23 Audits: Additional assessments raised by tax type.

StatLink https://doi.org/10.1787/888934310860

Figure 6.10. Additional assessments raised from audits undertaken by LTO/P as a percentage of additional assessments raised from all audits, 2020

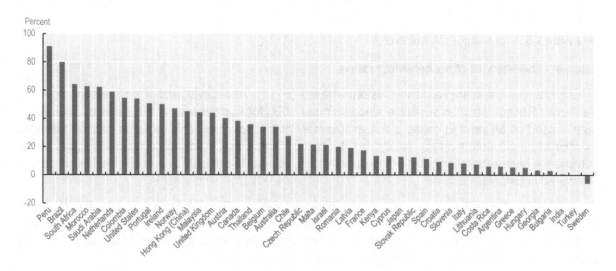

Source: Table D.9 Segmentation ratios: LTO/Ps.

StatLink ⟨⟩ https://doi.org/10.1787/888934310879

Moving audit work to a virtual environment

Traditionally, administrations apply a variety of different audit types including comprehensive audits, issue-oriented audits, inspections of books and records, and in-depth investigations of suspected tax fraud. Often those audits require the administration to visit the taxpayer's premises (so called field audits).

Advances in technology have led administrations to consider new ways of engaging with taxpayers during the audit process including the electronic submission of audit related documentation. This trend was accelerated as a result of the COVID-19 crisis as the closure of tax offices and the move to remote working for large numbers of tax officials changed how they approached audits.

This was observed in the 2021 OECD report *Tax Administration: Digital Resilience in the COVID-19 Environment* (OECD, 2021[6]) which noted of the 32 administrations covered by that report, close to ninety percent shifted parts of their field audit work to a virtual / digital environment. Moreover, 76% of those administrations plan to continue moving field audit work to a virtual/digital environment going forward. This is supported by an increased use of technology in audits which is helping drive efficiency. Box 6.6 highlights some leading practices, and the example from Estonia is of note as it is helping drive upstream compliance.

Box 6.6. Examples - Technology in audits

Chile – Tax radar

In Chile, the *Servicio de Impuestos Internos* (SII) is using data-driven decision making by providing, in the most intuitive way possible, large amounts of data for staff to use in their work. The Tax Radar dashboard aims to generate a view that allows staff to identify groups of relevant taxpayers on which the SII might not be carrying out control actions. The user can see the full-range (universe) of taxpayers and manipulate it through different institutional categories, such as global risk classification, monetary-impact for the tax system, type and size of business, current status and jurisdiction. It also incorporates different types of non-compliance, allowing the users to drill down on the information and establish different types of treatment action for the group or situation. The dashboard can also be used as a starting point to a more detailed analysis or as a knowledge management tool. This dashboard, and the analytics behind it, helps the SII save around 1 000 hours in analytical workload a month.

See Annex 6.A for supporting material.

Estonia - The e-service of tax behaviour rating

In Estonia, the Estonian Tax and Customs Board (ETCB) has developed a new e-service – Tax Behaviour Ratings which is available since summer 2020 for businesses. In this service, a variety of data is used as an input to create a risk assessment of the business. This includes data on turnover, number of employees, average salary, tax debts, tax compliance, and the company directors. A tax compliance behaviour rating is then calculated, which includes the risk of tax audit for each legal person registered in Estonia.

Taxpayers can then see themselves and their business partners through the eyes of the ETCB as well as comparing themselves with their peers. The taxpayer can also share their ratings with other users of the service, or publically, so that they can demonstrate they are a compliant business. This helps build trusted relationships and incentivise compliant behaviour.

(See Annex 6.A for links to supporting material.)

Georgia – Audit case management system

In order to automate and effectively implement tax audit processes, in 2018 the Revenue Service of the Ministry of Finance of Georgia launched the development of a new electronic audit system. The purpose of the system is:

- Effective Process Management and Monitoring - The system gathers all the audits in the Audit Department (both completed and ongoing) and the manager has the opportunity to receive complete information about the audit, according to the audit processes, including activities carried out within the framework of the tax inspection as well as the obtained and created documentation.

- Analysis and Feedback of Audit Results - A comprehensive analysis of completed tax audits is possible in the system, including an analysis of identified tax liabilities by areas of activity. It is also possible to analyse information in relation to the identified risks, which allows for further planning.

- Allocation of resources - Managers can see how many issues an auditor is inspecting, and the complexity of those issues. This can help in case allocation, as the system reflects the time spent by the auditor on the tasks performed.

Sources: Chile (2022), Estonia (2022) and Georgia (2022).

Tax crime investigations

Tax crime refers to a conduct that violates a tax law and can be investigated, prosecuted and sentenced under criminal procedures within the criminal justice system. There is a range of organisational approaches for conducting tax crime investigations and the ISORA 2021 survey looked at the responsibility for directing and conducting those investigations.

The information gathered through the ISORA 2021 survey shows that 55% of the tax administrations covered in this publication are involved in conducting tax crime investigations (Table A.36). The majority of those administrations have responsibility for both conducting and directing tax crime investigations, while the others have responsibility for solely conducting investigations, under the direction or authority of another agency, such as the police or public prosecutor (see Figure 6.11).

Box 6.7. Recently published OECD reports on Tax Crime

Fighting Tax Crime – The Ten Global Principles, Second Edition

First published in 2017, *Fighting Tax Crime - The Ten Global Principles* (OECD, 2021[7]) is the first comprehensive guide to fighting tax crimes. It sets out ten essential principles covering the legal, institutional, administrative, and operational aspects necessary for developing an efficient and effective system for identifying, investigating and prosecuting tax crimes, while respecting the rights of accused taxpayers. The second edition addresses new challenges, such as tackling professionals who enable tax and white-collar crimes, and fostering international co-operation in the recovery of assets. Drawing on the experiences of jurisdictions in all continents, the report also highlights successful cases relating to the misuse of virtual assets, complex investigations involving joint task forces, and the use of new technology tools to fight tax crimes and other financial crimes. The second edition is joined by a series of "country chapters", detailing jurisdictions' domestic tax crime enforcement frameworks as well as the progress made in implementing the Ten Global Principles.

Ending the Shell Game: Cracking down on the Professionals who enable Tax and White Collar Crimes

White collar crimes like tax evasion, bribery, and corruption are often concealed through complex legal structures and financial transactions facilitated by lawyers, accountants, financial institutions and other "professional enablers" of such crimes. These crimes have significant impacts on government revenue, public confidence and economic growth, including the recovery from COVID-19. The report *Ending the Shell Game: Cracking down on the Professionals who enable Tax and White Collar Crimes* (OECD, 2021[8]) highlights the damaging role played by professional enablers, and the importance of concerted domestic and international action in clamping down on them. Drawing from the experience from several jurisdictions, it also includes recommended counter-strategies for deterring, disrupting, investigating and prosecuting the professionals who enable tax and white collar crimes.

In the cases of administrations that do not have any responsibility for conducting tax crime investigations, this work is done by another agency, such as the police or public prosecutor. This could also be a specialist tax agency, established outside the tax administration.

Figure 6.11. Role of administrations in tax crime investigations, 2020

Percent of administrations

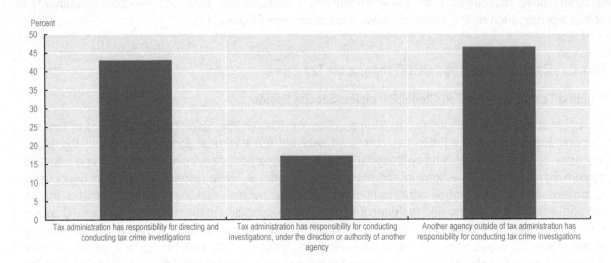

Note: In some jurisdictions, the organisational approach for tax crime investigations may depend on the tax offence or tax-related criminal proceedings. In those cases, an administration may have selected multiple answer options. This is why the percentages add up to more than 100%.
Source: Table A.36 Tax crime investigations: Role of the administration and number of cases.

StatLink 🔗 https://doi.org/10.1787/888934310898

Table 6.4 shows the total number of cases referred for prosecution during the fiscal year for the 32 administrations that have responsibility for conducting tax crime investigations. While the number of cases referred for prosecution was similar in 2018 and 2019, there was a significant reduction in the number of cases referred for prosecution during 2020.

This is also reflected in the jurisdiction level data, which shows that close to three quarters of administrations that have responsibility for conducting tax crime investigations referred fewer cases for prosecution in 2020 (see Table A.36).

Table 6.4. Tax crime investigation cases referred for prosecution

Year	No. of cases referred for prosecution during the fiscal year	Change in percent (compared to previous year)
2018	41 631	
2019	40 426	-2.9
2020	33 874	-16.2

Note: Only includes administrations that have responsibility.
Source: Table A.36 Tax crime investigations: Role of the administration and number of cases.

There could be many reasons for this reduction. This could include a genuine decline in cases, administrations reducing staff in this area as part of a wider reallocation of resources due to the pandemic, or the pandemic may imposed constraints on the ability to refer cases for prosecution. Future editions of this series will be able to identify if the reduction this year was a 'blip' caused by the pandemic or the start of a long-term trend.

Finding better ways to fight tax crime is a high priority as money laundering, corruption, terrorist financing, and other financial crimes can threaten the strategic, political and economic interests of jurisdictions. Tax administrations, as gatekeepers to a sound financial system, play a critical role in countering these activities and are in possession of information that could be crucial for a successful criminal tax investigation. Fighting tax crime requires improved transparency and greater efforts to harness the capacity of different government agencies, including across borders, to collectively deter, detect and prosecute these crimes through a whole of government approach and international co-operation, as Box 6.8 illustrates.

Box 6.8. Norway – Emerging risks

A threat assessment the Norwegian Tax Administration (NTA) made available in late 2021 showed increased risks of tax and work-related crime, post COVID-19. The digital shift has also contributed to the creation of new digital platforms used by criminals and professional enablers. Five main threats stand out: criminal networks; misuse of financial support schemes; work-related crime, professional enablers, and the opportunities of illegal activities through digitalisation. NTAs approach involves being prepared, cross-disciplinary collaboration, and as far as possible achieving real-time developments and changes.

Regarding criminal networks, NTA anticipate that these networks will use digital platforms to a greater extent in future as a means to carry out and coordinate their criminal activities. Serious crime is often systematic by nature. This may include cross-border activities in combination with other types of crime, and the use of other peoples "digital verified identities".

NTA have also seen that public registers are vulnerable and can be manipulated by criminal actors, for example via incorrect registrations and reporting. Some actors have and are expected to deliberately exploit the arrangements granting them payment deferrals before claiming insolvency. Different professional enablers such as lawyers, accountants and other roles within finance are considered to contribute to hiding assets or concealing the real ownership in connection with bankruptcy.

Source: Norway (2022).

References

OECD (2021), *Ending the Shell Game: Cracking down on the Professionals who enable Tax and White Collar Crimes*, OECD, Paris, https://www.oecd.org/tax/crime/ending-the-shell-game-cracking-down-on-the-professionals-who-enable-tax-and-white-collar-crimes.htm (accessed on 13 May 2022). [8]

OECD (2021), *Fighting Tax Crime – The Ten Global Principles, Second Edition*, OECD Publishing, Paris, https://doi.org/10.1787/006a6512-en. [7]

OECD (2021), "Tax Administration: Digital Resilience in the COVID-19 Environment", *OECD Policy Responses to Coronavirus (COVID-19)*, OECD Publishing, Paris, https://doi.org/10.1787/2f3cf2fb-en. [6]

OECD (2020), *Code of Conduct: Co-operation between tax administrations and sharing and gig economy platforms*, OECD, Paris, https://www.oecd.org/tax/forum-on-tax-administration/publications-and-products/code-of-conduct-co-operation-between-tax-administrations-and-sharing-and-gig-economy-platforms.pdf (accessed on 13 May 2022). [4]

OECD (2020), *Model Rules for Reporting by Platform Operators with respect to Sellers in the Sharing and Gig Economy*, OECD, Paris, https://www.oecd.org/tax/exchange-of-tax-information/model-rules-for-reporting-by-platform-operators-with-respect-to-sellers-in-the-sharing-and-gig-economy.htm (accessed on 13 May 2022). [3]

OECD (2019), *The Sharing and Gig Economy: Effective Taxation of Platform Sellers : Forum on Tax Administration*, OECD Publishing, Paris, https://doi.org/10.1787/574b61f8-en. [2]

OECD (2017), *The Changing Tax Compliance Environment and the Role of Audit*, OECD Publishing, Paris, https://doi.org/10.1787/9789264282186-en. [1]

OECD (2016), *Advanced Analytics for Better Tax Administration: Putting Data to Work*, OECD Publishing, Paris, https://doi.org/10.1787/9789264256453-en. [5]

Annex 6.A. Links to supporting material (accessed on 13 May 2022)

- Box 6.1. – Italy: Link to a document with more details on the new methodology for the estimation of the VAT gap: https://www.oecd.org/tax/forum-on-tax-administration/database/b.6.1-italy-vat-gap-estimation.pdf

- Box 6.2. – Argentina: Link to a presentation providing additional information on the Simple and Pro-Forma VAT Tax Return: https://www.oecd.org/tax/forum-on-tax-administration/database/b.6.2-argentina-simple-and-pro-forma-vat-tax-return.pdf

- Box 6.2. – France: Link to a presentation that explains more about the process of detecting undeclared constructions: https://www.oecd.org/tax/forum-on-tax-administration/database/b.6.2-france-foncier-innovant.pdf

- Box 6.2. – Lithuania: Link to a document that contains more details regarding the project to increase transparency of second hand car transactions: https://www.oecd.org/tax/forum-on-tax-administration/database/b.6.2-lithuania-car-dealerships.pdf

- Box 6.2. – Spain: Link to a presentation with more detail regarding the project to analyse feedback from verification actions: https://www.oecd.org/tax/forum-on-tax-administration/database/b.6.2-spain-tax-audit-feedback.pdf

- Box 6.6. – Chile: Link to a video providing more details on the Tax Radar dashboard: https://www.youtube.com/watch?v=Aic6RTav5AM

- Box 6.6. – Estonia: Link to the tax administration's website on the e-service of tax behaviour ratings, including explanatory videos: https://www.emta.ee/en/business-client/e-services-training-courses/advice/what-tax-behaviour-ratings-tell-you

7 Collection

The collection of outstanding returns and payments is important for maintaining high levels of voluntary compliance and citizen's confidence in the overall tax system. This chapter comments on tax administration performance in managing the collection of outstanding debt, and describes the features of a modern tax debt collection function. It goes on to provide examples of approaches applied by administrations to prevent debt being incurred.

Introduction

The collection function involves engaging with, and potentially taking enforcement action against those who do not file a return on time, and/or do not make a payment when it is due. Even with the growth in pre-filled or no return approaches over past years (see Chapter 4), the filing of a tax return or declaration still remains the principal means by which a taxpayer's liability is established in the majority of jurisdictions participating in this publication. Although 2020 on-time filing rates averaged between 78% and 88%, around 100 million returns were not filed on time that year (see Chapter 4). It is important therefore that administrations continue to focus efforts on improving the timely collection of late and outstanding returns.

Looking at the collection of late payments, all but one administration participating in the survey report staff resources being devoted to taking action to secure the payment of overdue tax payments (the Chilean tax administration reported not being responsible for debt collection; see Table A.8). Information provided by administrations in ISORA 2021, attributes around 11% of total staff numbers to the collection function (see Table D.4).

The legislative framework provides tax officials with powers that enable them to undertake certain actions in relation to the management of debt, the collection of amounts overdue and the enforcement actions that can be taken against delinquent debtors. The 2019 edition in this series had a section summarising the availability of such management, collection and enforcement powers and their usage by tax administrations (OECD, 2019[1]). Since then the ISORA survey did not take a closer look at this topic. However, it is fair to assume that the availability and usage of such powers has not significantly changed.

This chapter:

- Takes a brief look at the features of a modern tax debt collection function and the elements of a successful tax debt management strategy;
- Comments on tax administration performance in managing the collection of outstanding debt;
- Provides examples of preventive approaches to debt being incurred; and
- Examines the immediate impact of the COVID-19 pandemic on debt levels, which is likely to be a trend touching future editions of this series.

Features of a debt collection function

To maintain high levels of voluntary compliance and confidence in the tax system, administrations must ensure that their debt collection approaches are both "fit for purpose" and meet taxpayer's expectations of how the system will be administered. This means not only taking firm action against taxpayers that knowingly do not comply, but also using more customer service style approaches where taxpayers want to meet their obligations but for understandable reasons, such as short-term cash-flow issues, are not able to do so. Increasingly, tax administrations are taking an end-to-end or systems view of their processes and researching the reasons why returns may not been filed or payments made. They are also using information about the taxpayer's previous history, to identify patterns and/or anomalies.

The 2014 report *Working Smarter in Tax Debt Management* (OECD, 2014[2]) provided an overview of the modern tax debt collection function, describing the essential features as:

- *Advanced analytics* – that make it possible to use all the information tax administrations have about taxpayers to accurately target debtors with the right intervention at the right time.
- *Treatment strategies* – the collection function needs a range of interventions, from those designed to minimise the risk of people becoming indebted, to support taxpayers to make payments and to take appropriate enforcement measures where appropriate.
- *Outbound call centres* – which make it possible to efficiently pursue a large number of debts.

- *Organisation* – debt collection is a specialist function and is usually organised as such. The right performance measures and a continuous improvement approach help drive desired outcomes.

- *Cross border debts* – the proper and timely use of international assistance is crucial, particularly the "Assistance in Collection Articles" in agreements between jurisdictions.

The 2019 report *Successful Tax Debt Management: Measuring Maturity and Supporting Change* (OECD, 2019[3]) provides further insights into the elements of a successful tax debt management strategy, setting out four strategic principles that tax administrations may wish to consider when setting their strategy for tax debt management. These principles focus on the timing of interventions in the tax debt cycle, from consideration of measures to prevent tax debt arising in the first place, via early and continuous engagement with taxpayers before enforcement measures, to effective and proportionate enforcement and realistic write-off strategies. The underlying premise for these principles is that focusing on tackling debt early, and ideally before it has arisen, is the best means to minimise outstanding tax debt. The report also contains an overview of a *Tax Debt Management Maturity Model* and a compendium of successful tax debt management initiatives.

Box 7.1. Examples - Tools to advance debt management

Argentina – Risk profiling

Argentina has created a risk profile system called SIPER, which performs a monthly automatic categorization of the entire Taxpayer Register of the Federal Administration of Public Revenue (AFIP). SIPER identifies non-compliant taxpayers, and risk categories are allocated from low risk to high risk, based upon different types of controls (called deviations) that identify formal, material and judicial breaches registered in AFIP's systems.

The system notifies taxpayers of the category they were allocated, including the reasons, and gives taxpayers the chance to correct any errors using different data. One of the most important uses of SIPER is identifying the category "Distinctive non-compliance management", which contains 86% of debt. This allows for focused administrative collection measures on taxpayers with the highest tax risk, and the beginning of judicial proceedings in a shorter time.

The aim of SIPER is to foster the idea in taxpayers that compliance is the best option, which brings more benefits in the long term as non-compliance entails a higher cost.

Canada – Tailoring services

The Canada Revenue Agency (CRA) risk assessment process determines the allocation of accounts at the appropriate level based on a risk score. This initiative ensures that accounts are directed to specific workloads and processed according to associated strategies. The CRA has already developed strategies that segment collection accounts with specific stakeholder interactions, such as insolvency-related files. There are additional opportunities to segment based on debtor and debt characteristics. The CRA will segment portions of their inventories to group accounts and develop expertise among the collectors in how to best resolve these accounts.

Segmenting accounts based on common characteristics will allow for a more targeted approach to the collection of these debts. For instance, by segmenting deceased accounts, which are a specialty workload and of a sensitive nature, they will be handled in a different manner where the CRA will assist the trustees of the estate to resolve the debt and obtain a clearance certificate. The ultimate outcome for segmenting accounts is to have them assigned to the right individual at the right time, avoiding inventory backlogs with accounts that could be resolved at an earlier stage of the collections continuum.

United States - Optimising Collection Delivery and Selection

In 2021, the Internal Revenue Service's (IRS) Collection organisation revamped its process for determining the best work stream for a particular case by expanding the use of predictive models into routing decisions. The objective was to optimise assignment of Collection inventory to treatment streams (within operational constraints), allocate productive inventory more effectively, and identify unproductive inventory more quickly. IRS Collection has a suite of predictive models that integrates behavioural insights with the vast amount of available tax administrative data, to better anticipate the complexity and the level of effort that will be required to resolve a case. The models were built using logistic regression. They help predict the likelihood a taxpayer will resolve their liabilities by payment or payment agreements, the risk of future non-compliance, and the expected amount of payments. As the models are utilised, their performance is continually evaluated, and refinements can be made to improve their accuracy and functionality over time.

Case routing uses several predictive models to optimise three different factors: future compliance, dollars collected and case resolution, and having several factors included in the routing decision provides flexibility in weighting factors based on strategic priorities and inventory levels. As the use of predictive models expands, this provides a foundation upon which future analytical capabilities can be built.

Sources: Argentina (2022), Canada (2022) and the United States (2022).

Performance in collecting outstanding debt

The total amount of outstanding arrears at fiscal year-end remains very large, in the region of EUR 2.3 trillion. For survey and comparative analysis purposes, "total arrears at year-end" is defined as the total amount of tax debt and debt on other revenue for which the tax administration is responsible that is overdue for payment at the end of the fiscal year. This includes any interest and penalties. The term also includes arrears whose collection has been deferred (for example, as a result of payment arrangements).

The total amount of "Collectable arrears" at fiscal year-end was around EUR 900 billion. Collectable arrears is defined as the total arrears figure less any disputed amounts, or amounts that are not legally recoverable. It also includes arrears which are unable to be collected, but where write-off action has not yet occurred.

As a result, and despite efforts to make data comparable, care needs to be taken when comparing specific data points as the administration of taxation systems and administrative practices differ between jurisdictions. Care also needs to be taken because of the impact of the COVID-19 pandemic, which is likely impacting on this year's figures. This is because many governments took action to support individuals and businesses as part of the pandemic by extending payment terms, or suspending collection of outstanding debt. This may well be a major factor in the increase in collectable arrears between 2019 and 2020 may be a result of this. (CIAT/IOTA/OECD, 2020[4]). Future editions of this series will likely continue to reflect the impact of these actions as tax administrations slowly return to pre-pandemic activities.

In 2020, the average ratio for total year-end arrears to net revenue collected was 37% (see Table D.19). As in past years, it remains heavily influenced by the very large ratios of a small number of jurisdictions that show ratios above 90%. If these jurisdictions are removed, the average reduces to around 15% of net revenue (see Figures 7.1 and 7.2 as well as Table D.19).

Table 7.1. Average arrears ratios

Arrears ratio	2018	2019	2020	Change in percent (between 2019 – 2020)
Total year-end arrears as percentage of net revenue collected (50 jurisdictions)	28.2	27.9	34.7	+24.4
Total year-end collectable arrears as percentage of total year-end arrears (41 jurisdictions)	51.8	52.5	55.3	+5.3

Note: The table shows average arrears ratios for those jurisdictions that were able to provide the information for the years 2018, 2019 and 2020. The number of jurisdictions for which data was available is shown in parenthesis. Data for Bulgaria was excluded from the calculation of the average for the 'total year-end arrears as a percentage of net revenue collected' as its data for the three years was not comparable (see Table A.31).
Source: Table D.19 Arrears: Closing stock, collectible arrears, and arrears relating to state owned enterprises.

When comparing 2020 with 2019 a significant increase in total year-end arrears to net revenue collected is visible. While there was almost no change between 2019 and 2018, during 2020 – the year of the pandemic – the ratio increased on average by more than 20 percent (see Table 7.1). Further, the jurisdiction level data shows that in 2020 the 'total arrears to net revenue collected' ratio increased in around 85% of jurisdictions (see Table D.19).

Looking at collectable tax arrears, the 2020 data for 41 jurisdictions shows that on average 55% of the total arrears are considered collectable. That is an increase of 5% compared to 2019 (see Table 7.1). However, Figure 7.3 illustrates well the differences between jurisdictions: in some jurisdictions almost all arrears are considered collectable, while in others almost all arrears are considered not collectable.

Figure 7.1. Total year-end arrears as a percent of total net revenue, 2020

Administrations with a ratio above 90%

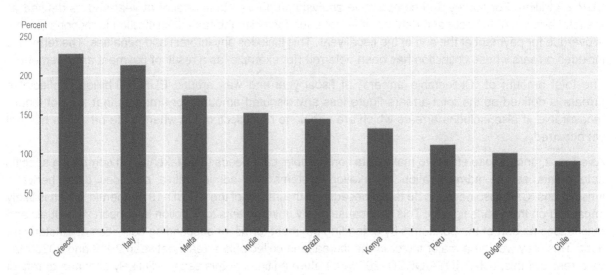

Source: Table D.19 Arrears: Closing stock, collectable arrears, and arrears relating to state owned enterprises.

StatLink https://doi.org/10.1787/888934310917

Figure 7.2. Total year-end arrears as a percent of total net revenue, 2020

Administrations with a ratio below 90%

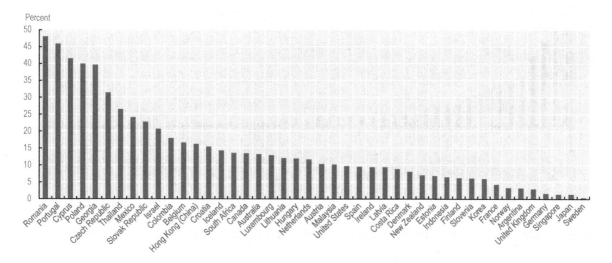

Source: Table D.19 Arrears: Closing stock, collectable arrears, and arrears relating to state owned enterprises.

StatLink https://doi.org/10.1787/888934310936

Figure 7.3. Total year-end collectable arrears as percentage of total year-end arrears, 2020

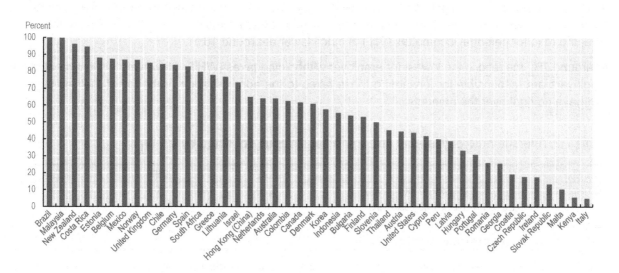

Source: Table D.19 Arrears: Closing stock, collectable arrears, and arrears relating to state owned enterprises.

StatLink https://doi.org/10.1787/888934310955

Figure 7.4. Movement of total arrears between 2019 and 2020

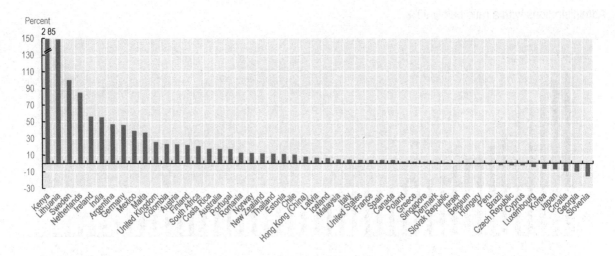

Note: The figure does not include data for Bulgaria as its data for the years 2019 and 2020 was not comparable (see Table A.31).
Source: Table D.21 Arrears: Year-on-year Change.

StatLink ᨆᨓ https://doi.org/10.1787/888934310974

Figure 7.4 show the change of total year-end arrears between 2019 and 2020. In absolute numbers, the total year-end arrears increased in 39 out of 51 jurisdictions that were able to provide the information.

In looking at the amount of arrears for the main tax types (see Table 7.2), it seems that individuals are more likely to pay on time than businesses. The average ratio of corporate income tax (CIT) arrears to CIT net revenue collected is around 35% and the ratio for value added taxes (VAT) is around 30%. At the same time, the ratio for personal income tax (PIT) is much lower at around 16%.

At around 7%, the ratio is the lowest for employer withholding taxes (WHT). However, this is expected, as employers are responsible for forwarding those taxes to the administration on behalf of their employees and have no right over the amounts.

Table 7.2. Average ratio of year-end arrears to net revenue collected by tax type

Tax type	2018	2019	2020
CIT arrears as percentage of CIT collected (41 jurisdictions)	29.2	31.0	34.9
PIT arrears as percentage of PIT collected (43 jurisdictions)	16.1	14.1	15.5
Employer WHT arrears as percentage of PIT collected (34 jurisdictions)	7.2	6.5	7.2
VAT arrears as percentage of VAT collected (40 jurisdictions)	23.7	23.3	29.8

Note: The table shows the average ratios for jurisdictions that were able to provide the information for the years 2018, 2019 and 2020. The number of jurisdictions for which data was available is shown in parentheses. Data for Bulgaria was excluded from the calculation of the average for the total year-end arrears as a percentage of net revenue collected as its data for the three years was not comparable (see Table A.31). Further, because they would distort the averages, data for Greece was excluded in the calculation of the average for CIT and data for Malta was excluded in the calculation of the average for VAT.
Source: Table D.20 Arrears in relation to collection by tax type.

Preventive approaches

The range of actions undertaken by tax administrations to prevent debt from arising and to collect outstanding arrears continues to evolve. Advances in predictive modelling and experimental techniques as reported in the OECD report *Advanced Analytics for Better Tax Administration* (OECD, 2016[5]) and in the compendium of successful tax debt management practices contained in the OECD report *Successful Tax Debt Management: Measuring Maturity and Supporting Change* (OECD, 2019[3]) are helping many administrations better match interventions with taxpayer specific risk. The approaches used fall into one of the following categories:

- Predictive analytics, which tries to understand the likelihood of certain outcomes and, as regards debt collection, includes modelling the risk that an individual or company will fail to pay as well as models that attempt to assess the likelihood of insolvency or other payment problems.

- Prescriptive analytics, which is about predicting the likely impact of actions on taxpayer behaviour, so that tax administrations can select the right course of action for any chosen taxpayer or group of taxpayers. (OECD, 2016[5])

Many administrations are blending both practices and have trialled a variety of approaches aimed at changing "taxpayer behaviour." As pointed out in Chapter 5, close to 70% of administrations are using behavioural insight methodologies or techniques. These practices have the potential to transform the approach to tax debt as administrations move away from the 'one-size-fits-all' approaches (where it is cost-effective to do so) and instead try to identify:

- Which cases should be subject to an intervention;
- When to intervene (for example, even before a return or payment might be due); and
- Which type of action would achieve the best cost-benefit outcome.

Box 7.2 illustrates the approaches taken by some administrations.

Box 7.2. Examples – targeting interventions

Colombia - Portfolio prioritisation model

Machine learning has been used intensively in the banking sector for some time to estimate the prioritization rating for debt recovery, with models being used to estimate the probability of debt collection. The Colombia Tax and Customs Administration (DIAN) decided to use these models with the aim of increasing the amount of the recovered debt and doing so in the shortest possible time.

The methodology had two stages. In the first stage, a survey answered by experts within DIAN was conducted to determine the importance of eight factors in debt collection. From this survey, it was possible to establish the importance of each of these factors when prioritizing the portfolio. For the second stage, different algorithms were included in the model. The purpose of this model was to estimate the probability that a taxpayer pays the amount due. In terms of debt collection, according to preliminary estimates for the period February to July 2021, the model has helped in the recovery of approximately COP 3 billion.

United States - Notice redesign

The IRS has applied behavioural insights to enhance a number of collection notices to make them easier for taxpayers to comprehend and act upon, thereby improving the taxpayer experience and reducing the instances where the debt must be escalated to higher-cost treatments. Many of the redesigned notices include a quick response code which taxpayers can scan with their cell phone to be taken to pages on the IRS.gov website with additional resources and information.

Before being placed into production, notices are tested to determine their effectiveness in improving compliance outcomes. An efficient and repeatable process was used to develop and test the effectiveness of redesigned notices using randomized control trials. The IRS completed a series of pilot

---

tests to measure the benefit of redesigning collection notices and to identify the most effective version of each notice. It also tested various models of the notices to capture taxpayer reaction to different behavioural nudges.

Results from the completed tests showed that redesigned collection notices improved payment compliance, increased use of self-service tools, and reduced costs to IRS, pointing to the benefits of systemic implementation. The IRS estimate that these redesigned notices may increase annual collections by as much as USD 800 million. The redesign promotes the availability and ease-of-use of IRS online services, increasing awareness of alternatives to lengthy wait times on the phone and facilitating taxpayers' ability to engage with IRS through their preferred channel.

Sources: Colombia (2022) and the United States (2022).

References

CIAT/IOTA/OECD (2020), "Tax administration responses to COVID-19: Measures taken to support taxpayers", *OECD Policy Responses to Coronavirus (COVID-19)*, OECD Publishing, Paris, https://doi.org/10.1787/adc84188-en. [4]

OECD (2019), *Successful Tax Debt Management: Measuring Maturity and Supporting Change*, OECD, Paris, https://www.oecd.org/tax/forum-on-tax-administration/publications-and-products/successful-tax-debt-management-measuring-maturity-and-supporting-change.htm (accessed on 13 May 2022). [3]

OECD (2019), *Tax Administration 2019: Comparative Information on OECD and other Advanced and Emerging Economies*, OECD Publishing, Paris, https://doi.org/10.1787/74d162b6-en. [1]

OECD (2016), *Advanced Analytics for Better Tax Administration: Putting Data to Work*, OECD Publishing, Paris, https://doi.org/10.1787/9789264256453-en. [5]

OECD (2014), *Working Smarter in Tax Debt Management*, OECD Publishing, Paris, https://doi.org/10.1787/9789264223257-en. [2]

8 Disputes

Dispute prevention and resolution are essential features of tax systems. This chapter explores both issues by looking at the strategies put in place by tax administrations to resolve and prevent disputes efficiently and effectively.

Introduction

Taxpayer rights and obligations are frequently set out in law or taxpayer charters. Table 8.1 sets out some of the most commonly reported rights and obligations. Underpinning these rights and obligations is effective access to processes that allow taxpayers to challenge assessments and decisions. This safeguards taxpayer rights and ensures that appropriate checks and balances exist on the exercising of tax powers by administrations. At the same time, tax administrations and taxpayers should also strive to work together to prevent disputes from arising in the first place, thus reducing burdens and uncertainty for both parties.

Table 8.1. Taxpayer's rights and obligations

Right	Obligation
To be informed, assisted, and heard	To be honest
Of appeal	To be co-operative
To pay no more than the correct amount of tax	To provide accurate information and documents on time
Certainty	To keep records
Privacy	To pay taxes on time
Confidentiality and secrecy	

Source: OECD (2019), *Tax Administration 2019: Comparative Information on OECD and other Advanced and Emerging Economies*, https://doi.org/10.1787/74d162b6-en.

This chapter examines the dispute resolution and review mechanisms in the jurisdictions covered by this report, as well as their performance in this area, and explores their dispute prevention strategies.

Dispute resolution review mechanisms

All 58 jurisdictions covered in this report provide taxpayers with the right to challenge assessments. Almost all administrations report having an internal review mechanism in place, and a large majority of administrations provide taxpayers with the option to seek an independent review by an external body, which can help improve legal certainty for taxpayers while avoiding potentially lengthy and costly legal proceedings. For those administrations that offer both review mechanisms, approximately 70% require taxpayers to seek an internal review before their case can be reviewed by an external body (see Figure 8.1).

Figure 8.1. Dispute resolution: Available review mechanisms, 2020

Percent of administrations

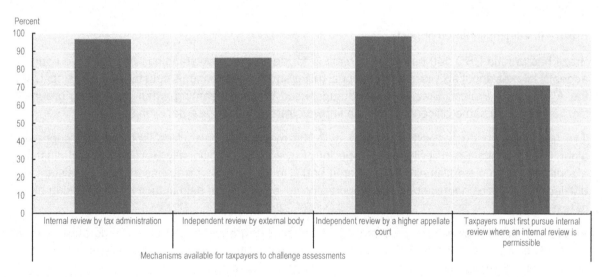

Source: Table A.37 Dispute resolution: Review procedures.

StatLink https://doi.org/10.1787/888934310993

Performance in dispute resolution

While tax administrations cannot generally control the timing of judicial processes, many of them are working on improving dispute resolution processes to make them quicker. These might include mediation or other non-judicial routes. The examples included in Box 8.2 illustrate how technological advances offer new possibilities for tax administrations to improve the efficiency of dispute resolution.

Box 8.2. Examples – Improving the efficiency of dispute resolution

Australia - Optimising Disputes through Self-Service (ODSS)

Currently, many objections the Australian Taxation Office (ATO) receives are incomplete, incorrect, or lack necessary supporting information and evidence. These consume significant time and resources, affecting the ATO's ability to resolve disputes in a timely and efficient manner. The Optimising Disputes through Self-Service (ODSS) project will initially focus on making an online objection form available to all clients across all ATO online services (in addition to the existing paper or fax methods).

ODSS also aims to provide taxpayers with decision assistance tools to help them choose the right pathway for resolving their issue. The contents of the form aims to be tailored based on taxpayer responses and taxpayers will be guided to ensure that all critical information is provided upfront. The online form empowers taxpayers to lodge objections correctly in the first instance, reducing unwanted delays for the taxpayer and unnecessary touchpoints, and reducing costs for both the taxpayer and the ATO.

In the longer term, the online objection form will also provide data which will be used to strengthen upfront risk assessment. Data entered by taxpayers in real-time will be used in conjunction with ATO data to identify the subject matter of the objection, and assess the complexity and priority. This will allow objections to be routed to the area and/or staff member with the most appropriate skills and capacity, and enable staff to apply greater focus to higher-risk and higher complexity disputes. ODSS will also facilitate the development of a risk engine to streamline decision making and ensure accuracy and consistency of case outcomes.

Brazil – Intelligent litigation project

Brazil has around USD 140 billion in tax waiting for decisions in outstanding administrative court tax appeals. It takes about six years for the appeal ruling and so the number is constantly increasing. Under the AI Litigation Project, Brazil employed supervised machine learning when distributing groups of similar files to the same officers, which is a known strategy to increase decision speed.

The first trials, conducted with a sample of 2 000 manually labeled files, showed that supervised algorithms can attain sensitivity and specificity of over 80%. Additionally Brazil employed clustering algorithms to complete files either in full or in part. On top of that, a web-based report assistant tool, entitled "ARiA", is being developed to support officers' analysis and help in their goal of reusing blocks of text.

ARiA's resources include the presentation of suggested groups of files and paragraphs and the highlighting of sentences that turned out to be important for the clustering process. Officers can label files and paragraphs, and the labels are used to improve future suggestions.

Sources: Australia (2022) and Brazil (2022).

Making effective adjustments to dispute resolution processes requires sound reporting and monitoring mechanisms, and many administrations are active in improving the level of management information available. As a result, this report contains performance information from approximately 90% of administrations.

Tables 8.2 and 8.3 compare the change between 2018 and 2020 in the number of review cases initiated and on hand at fiscal year-end, for both internal and external reviews. Between 2019 and 2020, the majority of administrations reported a reduction in the number of cases initiated and on hand at fiscal year-end. In relation to cases under internal review, this changes the results that can be observed over the period 2018 to 2019, where the majority of administrations reported increasing numbers.

Table 8.2. Dispute resolution: Change in number of cases initiated during the year

Percent of administrations that reported an increase or decrease in the number of cases initiated

Movement	Tax cases initiated under internal review procedure		Tax cases initiated under independent review by external bodies	
	Change between 2018 and 2019	Change between 2019 and 2020	Change between 2018 and 2019	Change between 2019 and 2020
Increase	51.0	39.2	44.4	27.3
Decrease	49.0	60.8	55.6	72.7

Source: Table A.38 Dispute resolution: Number of cases.

Table 8.3. Dispute resolution: Change in number of cases on hand at fiscal year-end

Percent of administrations that reported an increase or decrease in the number of cases on hand

Movement	Tax cases on hand under internal review procedure		Tax cases on hand under independent review by external bodies	
	Change between 2018 and 2019	Change between 2019 and 2020	Change between 2018 and 2019	Change between 2019 and 2020
Increase	63.3	44.9	48.8	34.1
Decrease	36.7	55.1	51.2	65.9

Source: Table A.38 Dispute resolution: Number of cases.

Figures 8.2 and 8.3 take a more detailed look at the jurisdiction level data and show the change between 2019 and 2020 in the number of review cases on hand at fiscal year-end, for both internal and external reviews. What is interesting to note are the significant increases in the number of review cases reported by a few jurisdictions.

At the same time, it should be pointed out that the volume of cases per jurisdiction varies significantly and where the number of cases is very low there can be significant fluctuations between years. This becomes more evident when looking at Figure 8.4, which highlights the wide differences between jurisdictions in the use of internal review procedures.

Figure 8.2. Internal review procedures: Change between 2019 and 2020 in the number of cases at fiscal year-end

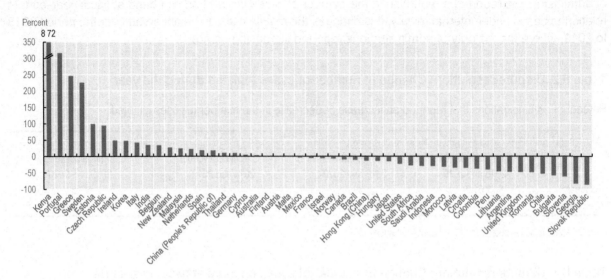

Source: Table A.38 Dispute resolution: Number of cases.

StatLink 🔳🔠 https://doi.org/10.1787/888934311012

Figure 8.3. Independent review by external bodies: Change between 2019 and 2020 in the number of cases at fiscal year-end

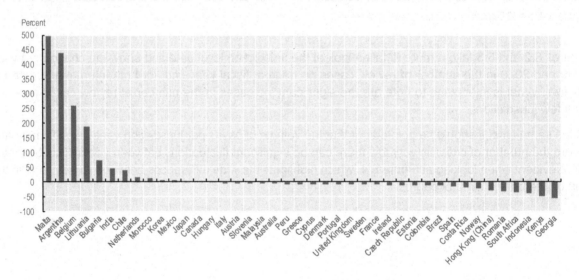

Source: Table A.38 Dispute resolution: Number of cases.

StatLink 🔳🔠 https://doi.org/10.1787/888934311031

Figure 8.4. Number of internal review cases initiated per 1 000 active PIT and CIT taxpayers, 2020

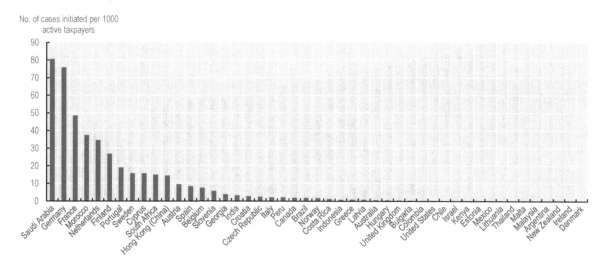

Note: For Saudi Arabia, the "No. of internal cases initiated during the FY per 1 000 active taxpayers" was put in relation to active VAT taxpayers.
Source: Table D.24 Administrative review cases and litigation.

StatLink https://doi.org/10.1787/888934311050

Different interpretations of tax law by taxpayers and the tax administration are a normal part of tax administration, and it is not uncommon for these differences to become subject to litigation, once the internal and external review procedures have been exhausted. Whilst tax administrations report that most disputes are resolved without the need for litigation, Figure 8.5 reports the performance of administrations for cases decided upon by the courts. It shows significant differences in the success rate of administrations, although for some jurisdictions the number of cases decided is very low, meaning results can fluctuate significantly between years.

Figure 8.5. Percentage of cases resolved in favour of the administration, 2020

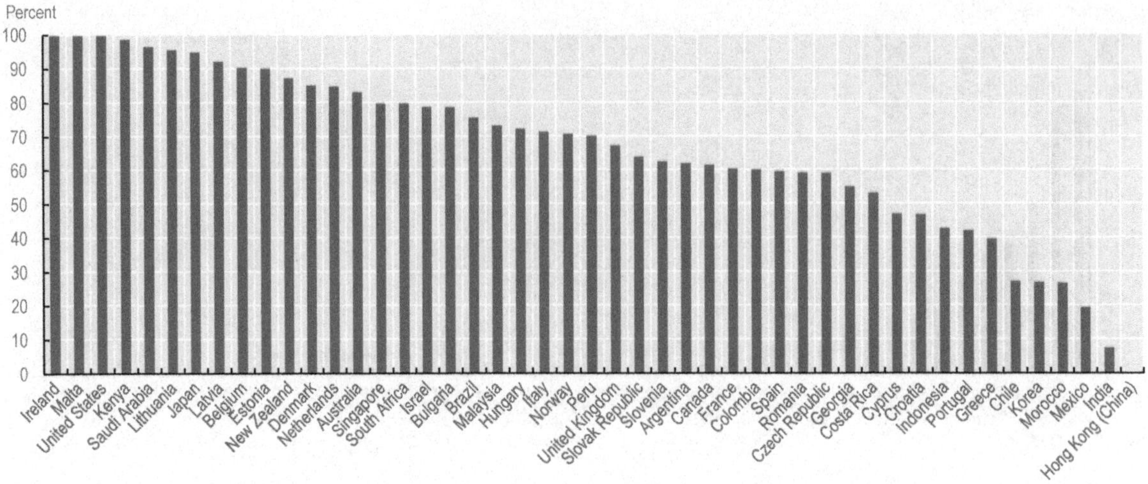

Note: Cases resolved in favour of the administration means those cases where the administration has been successful in more than 50% of the issues contested in each case. For France, Israel and Korea please see the notes in Table A.38.
Source: Table D.24 Administrative review cases and litigation.

StatLink https://doi.org/10.1787/888934311069

Dispute prevention

As disputes can be resource intensive processes, preventing them is the most effective strategy, and a key element in the dispute prevention framework is the provision of guidance and advice to taxpayers. Tax administrations often do this as part of their wider service strategy. This can include putting information and interactive tools on their website, publishing guidelines and taxpayer information briefs, and carrying out educational and business support initiatives.

In addition, many administrations offer specific dispute prevention mechanisms. For example, as noted in the chapter "Innovations in dispute resolution" in the 2019 edition of this series, the Australian Taxation Office explained their independent review of the technical merits of an audit case prior to the finalisation of the audit. The review aims to encourage earlier engagement to resolve disputes (OECD, 2019[1]). Initially this service was only available to large businesses with an annual turnover greater than AUD 250 million. However, following a successful pilot it has now been extended to small business taxpayers, i.e. taxpayers in business with income or turnover of less than AUD 10 million (Australian Taxation Office, 2022[2]).

Rulings

As shown in Table A.120 of the 2019 edition of this series (OECD, 2019[1]), as part of tax administrations' commitment to give taxpayers certainty of treatment, it is now common practice for administrations to set out how they will interpret the laws they administer, and how it will interpret the tax law in particular situations, through rulings:

- A **public ruling** is a published statement of how an administration will interpret provisions of the tax law in particular situations. They are generally published to clarify application of the law, especially where a large number of taxpayers may be impacted by particular provisions and/or where a provision has caused confusion or uncertainty. Typically, a public ruling is binding on the tax administration if the ruling applies to the taxpayer and the taxpayer relies upon it.

- A **private ruling** relates to a specific request from a taxpayer (or their tax representative) seeking greater certainty as to how the law would be applied by the tax administration in relation to a proposed or completed transaction(s). The objective of private rulings is to provide additional support and certainty to taxpayers on the tax consequences of more complex transactions.

Co-operative compliance programmes

Over the last few years, there has been an increasing focus on the use of co-operative arrangements to manage compliance and enhance tax certainty. These programmes often involve a more transparent relationship between tax administrations and taxpayers, and can involve more proactive approaches to resolving material tax risks. The concept of co-operative compliance has been the subject of several OECD reports, most recently *Co-operative Tax Compliance: Building Better Tax Control Frameworks* (OECD, 2016[3]).

As the operation of a co-operative compliance programme is resource intensive due to the high level of engagement between tax administration officials and taxpayers, traditionally those programmes were reserved for large companies. However, technological advances in risk assessment processes have led to a number of administrations applying this concept to other taxpayer groups (see Figure 8.6).

Figure 8.6. Existence of co-operative compliance approaches for different taxpayer segments, 2020

Percent of administrations that have such approaches

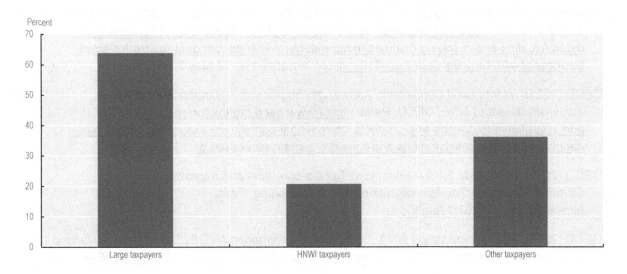

Source: Table A.50 Co-operative compliance approaches.

StatLink ᗰᔑᔑᖴᒪ https://doi.org/10.1787/888934311088

International Compliance Assurance Programme

The International Compliance Assurance Programme (ICAP) is a voluntary programme for a multilateral co-operative risk assessment and assurance process. It is designed to provide multinational enterprise groups (MNE groups) with increased tax certainty with respect to certain of their activities and transactions as long as they are willing to engage actively, openly and in a fully transparent manner. ICAP does not provide an MNE group with the legal certainty that may be achieved, for example, through an advance pricing arrangement (APA). However, it does give assurance when tax administrations participating in an MNE group's risk assessment consider covered risks to be low risk.[1] (OECD, 2021[4])

Joint audits

Another tool that can assist in preventing disputes is a joint audit where officials from two or more administrations join to form a single audit team which will examine issues or transactions of taxpayer(s) with cross-border business activities and in which the jurisdictions have a common or complementary interest. By collaborating it may be possible for the participating tax administrations to detect and address differences or potential disputes at an early stage. (OECD, 2019[5])

Note

[1]   See   www.oecd.org/tax/forum-on-tax-administration/international-compliance-assurance-programme.htm for more information (accessed on 13 May 2022).

References

Australian Taxation Office (2022), *Independent review for small businesses with turnover less than $10 million*, https://www.ato.gov.au/General/Dispute-or-object-to-an-ATO-decision/In-detail/Avoiding-and-resolving-disputes/Independent-review/Independent-review-for-small-businesses-with-turnover-less-than-$10-million/ (accessed on 13 May 2022).   [2]

OECD (2021), *International Compliance Assurance Programme – Handbook for tax administrations and MNE*, OECD, Paris, https://www.oecd.org/tax/forum-on-tax-administration/publications-and-products/international-compliance-assurance-programme-handbook-for-tax-administrations-and-mne-groups.htm (accessed on 13 May 2022).   [4]

OECD (2019), *Joint Audit 2019 – Enhancing Tax Co-operation and Improving Tax Certainty: Forum on Tax Administration*, OECD Publishing, Paris, https://doi.org/10.1787/17bfa30d-en.   [5]

OECD (2019), *Tax Administration 2019: Comparative Information on OECD and other Advanced and Emerging Economies*, OECD Publishing, Paris, https://doi.org/10.1787/74d162b6-en.   [1]

OECD (2016), *Co-operative Tax Compliance: Building Better Tax Control Frameworks*, OECD Publishing, Paris, https://doi.org/10.1787/9789264253384-en.   [3]

9 Budget and workforce

This chapter looks at the resources devoted to tax administrations and provides information on their workforce. It sets out how administrations are responding to the post-pandemic workplace and how they maintain their capability while managing a workforce that in general terms is reducing in size and on average is getting older. It also explores how technology is helping tax administrations empower their workforce to deliver better solutions for taxpayers as well as provide more flexibility for the administration and its employees.

Introduction

Central to a tax administration meeting its role in collecting revenue and providing services to citizens and businesses, is sufficient financial resources and a skilled workforce that can deliver quality outputs efficiently and effectively. The first part examines the financial resources available to tax administrations, and how they are spent. The second part provides information on tax administrations' workforce, and how the COVID-19 pandemic has reshaped working practices.

Budget and information and communication technology

Operating expenditures

The overall level of resources devoted to tax administration is an important and topical issue for most governments, external stakeholders, and of course tax administrations themselves. While the budgetary approaches differ, in most jurisdictions the budget allocated is tied to the delivery of performance outputs which are outlined in an annual business plan.

When looking at the budget figures, slightly more than two-thirds of tax administrations report an increase in their operational expenditure between the years 2019 and 2020. This is fewer administrations than over the period 2018 to 2019, where three-quarters reported an increase (see Table 9.1).

However, this data should be treated with caution. While on paper a significant number of administrations saw increases in their budget, this does not take into the account the increases in responsibilities that many administrations are reporting, especially as a result of additional pandemic responsibilities, as well as any inflationary pressures.

Table 9.1. Changes in operating expenditures

Percent of administrations

Change	Between 2018 and 2019 (based on data for 54 administrations)	Between 2019 and 2020 (based on data for 55 administrations)
Increase in operating expenditure	75.9	69.1
Decrease in operating expenditure	24.1	30.9

Source: Secretariat calculations based on Table A.7.

This issue is compounded as a significant part of the budgets is needed for salary costs, accounting for on average 73% of operating budgets annually (see Figure 9.1). Any increases in budgets can be rapidly consumed by salary increases, which may be a contractual obligation. This mix of greater responsibility, and pressured budgets, is driving tax administrations to find innovative approaches, often using technology, so they can meet budgetary constraints, continue to deliver efficient services to taxpayers, and focus on the relevant compliance risks.

As tax administrations reflect on the working practices established as part of the pandemic response, the impact of longer term hybrid or remote working is also being considered. This was explored in more detail in the OECD report *Tax Administration: Towards sustainable remote working in a post COVID-19 environment* (OECD, 2021[1]), and the examples in Box 9.1 set out some of the new working practices being adopted after the pandemic.

Box 9.1. Examples - New working practices

Canada – Transitioning to a hybrid workplace

Before the COVID-19 pandemic, over 90% of Canada Revenue Agency (CRA) employees worked in the office full-time. Since the pandemic, these figures have been reversed and the majority of employees are working from home. While keeping employees safe and healthy during the public health crisis was the catalyst for this radical shift, employees have also expressed a desire for more flexible working arrangements to continue.

To establish a consistent approach to implementing a hybrid model of working at the national level, business requirements were examined, balancing efficient programme delivery with providing employees flexibility. The approach was based on five guiding principles (well-being, stewardship, service to Canadians, productivity, and security), and was discussed in-depth across the organisation. As a result of these discussions, mandatory and discretionary in-office drivers were established to determine where work should be performed, based on the tasks being completed.

A multi-disciplinary team is guiding the CRA transition to a hybrid model of work, which is defined as working remotely, working on-site or a combination of both depending on business and operational needs. By centralising and implementing flexible management, planning and coordination mechanisms, the CRA has initiated this large-scale transformation affecting its workforce, worksites, workflows, and overall approach to conducting work. This approach is at the forefront of government-wide discussions and is being promoted as a model for other government departments.

Chile - Mobility Plan

At the beginning of the COVID-19 pandemic, *Servicio de Impuestos Internos* (SII) implemented a teleworking protocol to facilitate the work of their employees from their homes. It is now being piloted how this can continue after the pandemic, on a voluntary basis for certain staff.

Two directorates are in the pilot, the Administrative Directorate and the Directorate for Human Resources Development, to explore the impact of staff 50% teleworking and 50% in the office. SII anticipates that this could bring cost savings in reduced office space as well as savings in office supplies and furniture, maintenance, electricity; air conditioning and printing. SII also recognises that teleworking will also have additional expenses, e.g. supply of home office furniture and IT equipment, associated costs of electricity and internet as well as training and education in the use and management of remote information.

SII is already seeing benefits from this pilot around flexibility, productivity and efficiency, improved services to taxpayers and better work life balance for staff.

See Annex 9.A for supporting material.

Portugal - Innovations in working practices

Investment in IT infrastructures has been a priority in *Autoridade Tributária e Aduaneira* (AT) not only in terms of provision of digital tools but also to ensure that levels of performance and well-being of the workforce are maintained.

In order to realise a fully supported workforce and digital workplace strategy, AT invested in remote access for employees, laptops and different communication technology options. In addition, there was development and training in new communication skills, and improvement in document management software in order to replace paper with digital alternatives.

This digitisation has led AT to focus particularly on issues related to information security and cybersecurity, and reinforcing mechanisms like Multifactor Authentication. In addition, processes have been enhanced to detect, respond and recover from information security incidents.

Sources: Canada (2022), Chile (2022) and Portugal (2022).

Components of tax administration operating expenditure

As stated above, the largest reported component of tax administration operating budgets is staff costs, with salary alone accounting for on average 73% of operating budgets annually (see Figure 9.1). Another important component is the operating cost for information and communication technology (ICT). On average this accounts for 10% of operating expenditure, with a few jurisdictions reporting ICT expenditure above 20% of their total operating expenditure (see Table D.3). The averages for both items (salary and ICT) have remained stable over the past years.

Capital expenditure

Capital expenditure makes-up about 4% of total expenditure on average but varies significantly between administrations. A few administrations report figures below 1% while others report figures above 10% (see Table A.7).

Cost of collection

It has become a fairly common practice for tax administrations to compute and publish (e.g. in their annual reports) a "cost of collection" ratio as a surrogate measure of their efficiency / effectiveness. The ratio is computed by comparing the annual expenditure of a tax administration, with the net revenue collected over the course of a fiscal year. Given the many similarities in the taxes administered by tax administrations, there has been a natural tendency by observers to make comparisons of "cost of collection" ratios across jurisdictions. Such comparison have to be treated with a high degree of caution, for reasons explained in Box 9.2.

In practice there are a number of factors that may influence the cost/revenue relationship, but which have nothing to do with relative efficiency or effectiveness. Examples of such factors and variables include macroeconomic changes as well as differences in revenue types administered. These factors are further elaborated in Box 9.2.

Despite those factors, the "cost of collection" ratio is included in this report for two reasons:

1. The "cost of collection" ratio is useful for administrations to track as a domestic measure as it allows them to see the trend over time of their work to collect revenue and, as pointed out in Box 9.2, they may be able to account for the main factors that can influence the ratio; and

2. The inclusion of the "cost of collection" ratio and the accompanying comments set out in Box 9.2. can serve as a prominent reminder to stakeholders of the difficulties and challenges in using the easily calculated "cost of collection" ratio for international comparison.

Figure 9.2 illustrates the movement in the "cost of collection" ratios between 2019 and 2020 for the administrations included in this report. It shows that eighty percent of the administrations had increasing ratios, incontrast to the close to sixty percent of the administrations which had decreasing ratios over the period 2018 to 2019. However, as mentioned in Box 9.2, the chart and the underlying figures have to be interpreted with great care.

Figure 9.1. Salary cost as a percent of operating expenditure, 2020

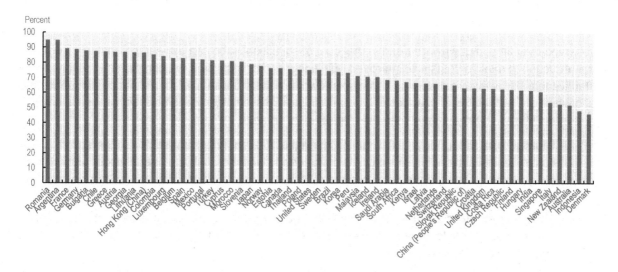

Source: Table D.3 Resource ratios

StatLink https://doi.org/10.1787/888934311107

Figure 9.2. Movement in "cost of collection" ratios between 2019 and 2020

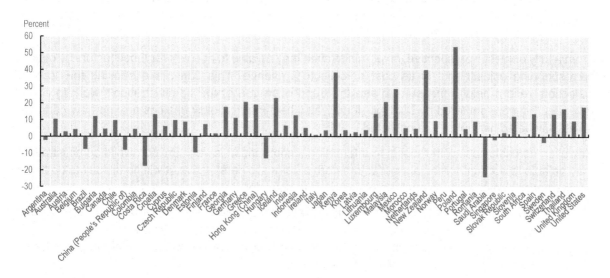

Note: When interpreting this chart the factors mentioned in Box 9.2 should be taken into account. Data for Israel and Turkey has been excluded, see notes in Table A.7.
Source: Table D.3 Resource ratios.

StatLink https://doi.org/10.1787/888934311126

Box 9.2. Difficulties and challenges in using the "cost of collection" ratio as an indicator of efficiency and/or effectiveness

Observed over time, a downward trend in the "cost of collection" ratio can appear to constitute evidence of a reduction in relative costs (i.e. improved efficiency) and/or improved tax compliance (i.e. improved effectiveness). However, experience has also shown that there are many factors that can influence the ratio which are **not** related to changes in a tax administrations' efficiency and/or effectiveness and which render this statistic highly unreliable in the international context:

- **Changes in tax policy**: Tax policy changes are an important factor in determining the cost/revenue relationship. In theory, a policy decision to increase the overall tax burden should, all other things being equal, improve the ratio by a corresponding amount, but this has nothing to do with improved operational efficiency or effectiveness.

- **Macroeconomic changes**: Significant changes in rates of economic growth etc. or inflation over time are likely to impact on the overall revenue collected by the tax administration and the cost/revenue relationship.

- **Abnormal expenditure of the tax administration**: From time to time, a tax administration may be required to undertake an abnormal level of investment (e.g. the building of a new information technology infrastructure or the acquisition of more expensive new accommodation). Such investments are likely to increase overall operating costs over the medium term, and short of offsetting efficiencies which may take longer to realise, will impact on the cost/ revenue relationship.

- **Changes in the scope of revenues collected**: From time to time, governments decide to shift responsibility for the collection of particular revenues from one agency to another which may impact the cost/revenue relationship.

From a fully domestic perspective, an administration may be able to account for those factors by making corresponding adjustments to its cost or collected revenue. This can make tracking the "cost of collection" ratio a helpful measure to see the trend over time of the administration's work to collect revenue. If it were gathered by tax type, it may also help inform policy choices around how particular taxes may be administered and collected.

However, its usefulness with respect to international comparison is very limited. While administrations may be able to account for the above factors from a domestic perspective, it will be difficult to do this at an international level as such analysis would have to consider:

- **Differences in tax rates and structure**: Rates of tax and the actual structure of taxes will all have a bearing on aggregate revenue and, to a lesser extent, cost considerations. For example, comparisons of the ratio involving high-tax jurisdictions and low-tax jurisdictions are hardly realistic given their widely varying tax burdens.

- **Differences in the range and nature of revenues administered**: There are a number of differences that can arise here. In some jurisdictions, more than one major tax authority may operate at the national level, or taxes at the federal level may be predominantly of a direct tax nature, while indirect taxes may be administered largely by separate regional/state authorities. In other jurisdictions, one national authority will collect taxes for all levels of government, i.e. federal, regional and local governments. Similar issues arise in relation to the collection of social insurance contributions.

- **Differences in the range of functions undertaken**: The range of functions undertaken by tax administrations can vary from jurisdiction to jurisdiction. For example, in some jurisdictions the tax administration is also responsible for carrying out activities not directly related to tax administration (e.g. the administration of certain welfare benefits or national population registers), while in others some tax-related functions are not carried out by the tax administration (e.g. the enforcement of debt collections). Further, differences in societal views may influence what an administration does, how it can operate and what services is has to offer. The latter may have a particularly significant impact on the cost/revenue relationship.

Finally, it should be pointed out that the "cost of collection" ratio ignores the revenue potential of a tax system, i.e. the difference between the amount of tax actually collected and the maximum potential revenue. This is particularly relevant in the context of international comparisons – administrations with similar cost/revenue ratios can be some distance apart in terms of their relative effectiveness.

Information and communication technology

On average ICT expenditure accounts for about 10% of operating expenditure. However, reported levels of ICT expenditure vary enormously between administrations. For those administrations able to provide ICT-related cost, around 40% reported an annual operating ICT expenditure exceeding 10% of the administration's total operating expenditure in 2020 and another 30% reported figures between 5% and 10% (see Table D.3). While some of this variation can be explained by the different sourcing and business approaches, some cannot and point, at least on the surface, to expenditure levels that maybe somewhat below the support needed to provide the rapidly changing electronic and digital services administrations are increasingly being called upon to deliver.

As regards the operational ICT solutions (i.e. solutions that are used to fulfil the tax administration's mandate and include systems for registration, return processing, payment processing and auditing), almost all tax administrations report using custom built ICT solutions, while 55% report also using commercial-off-the-shelf (COTS) solutions (see Figure 9.3).

Figure 9.3. Basis of ICT solutions of tax administrations, 2020

Percent of administrations that have such solutions

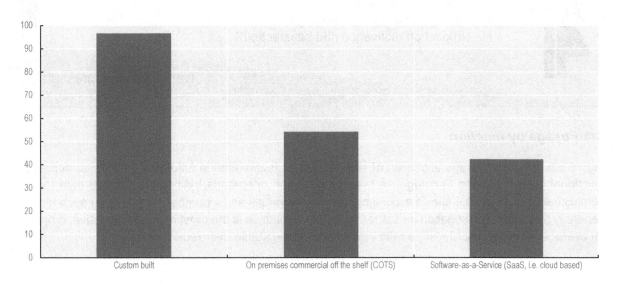

Source: Table A.9. Information and communication technology (ICT) solutions of the tax administration.

StatLink https://doi.org/10.1787/888934311145

In addition, around 40% of the administrations report using software-as-a-service (SaaS) solutions. These are software licensing models where the tax administration pays for a subscription license and the cost depends on the usage. The software is installed on third party computers, not on tax administration computers, and is accessed by users via the internet. One of the main barriers to adopting SaaS more widely, is the storage of sensitive tax data on these third party systems. As more legislative and technological solutions are identified, including regarding the encryption of data, it is possible the use of SaaS will increase.

Workforce

In 2020, the administrations included in this report employed approximately 1.7 million staff (see Table A.8) making the effective and efficient management of the workforce critical to good tax administration. Having a competent, professional, productive and adaptable workforce is at the heart of most administrations' human resource planning. With salary costs averaging more than 70% of operating expenditures, any significant budget change invariably impacts staff numbers.

The "double pressure" created from reduced budgets and technology change, mentioned in the 2017 edition (OECD, 2017[2]) (see also Figure 9.4), continues to be a significant management issue for most administrations. The challenge is compounded for some administrations which, due to contract restrictions or government mandates, may find it difficult to strategically down-size their operations other than through the non-replacement of staff who leave of their own accord.

Figure 9.4. Double pressure on the workforce

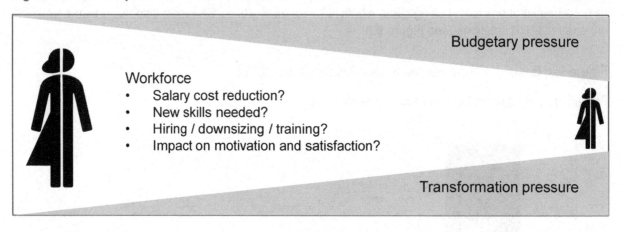

Staff usage by function

Figure 9.5 provides average allocation of staff resources (expressed in full-time equivalents) across four functional groupings used to categorise tax administration operations.[1] While the detailed data for each administration in Table D.4 shows a significant spread of values and a number of outliers for each function, generally the "audit, investigation and other verification" function is the most resource intensive, employing on average thirty percent of staff, a ratio that has remained stable over recent years.

Figure 9.5. Staff usage by function, 2020

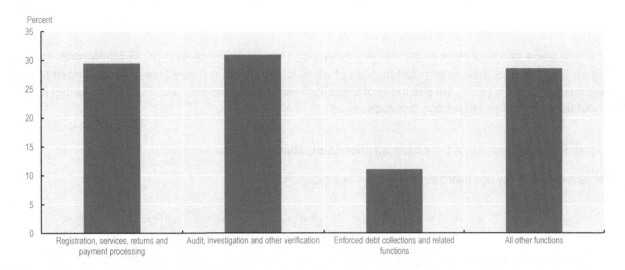

Note: Excluding administrations that were unable to provide the break-down for all functions.
Source: Table D.4. Staff allocation by function and location.

StatLink ▄▅▆ https://doi.org/10.1787/888934311164

Staff metrics

ISORA 2021 also gathered key data concerning the age profiles, length of service, gender distribution and educational qualifications of tax administration staff: see Tables D.6 to D.8 and A.11 to A.14. In interpreting this data, there are two main considerations to bear in mind:

- combined tax and customs administrations were allowed to use their total workforce for answering the underlying survey questions as it may be difficult for them to separate the characteristics of the tax and customs workforce.

- Since ISORA 2020, staff metrics information is collected for the total number of staff, whereas in previous ISORA rounds (i.e. ISORA 2016 and 2018) staff metrics information was collected for permanent staff only. Trend analysis comparing staff metrics across the different ISORA surveys should therefore be conducted with caution. In particular, for administrations that employ a significant number of non-permanent staff, this change in methodology may cause a shift in staff-metric-percentages that is not based on regular staff fluctuations but rather a result of including a different group of staff.

Age profiles

While there are significant variations between the age profiles of tax administration staff (see Table D.6), it is interesting to see that there are also differences when viewed across different regional groupings. This may be the result of a complex mix of cultural, economic, and sociological factors (e.g. economic maturity, recruitment, remuneration, and retirement policies).

Figure 9.6 illustrates that staff are generally younger in administrations in the regional groupings of "Asia-Pacific" and "Middle East and Africa" where, on average, around one third of staff are below 35 years of age, whereas in the "Americas" and "Europe" this percentage drops to below twenty percent. At the same time, administrations in the "Americas" and "Europe" have a large percentage of staff older than 54 years.

Looking at the jurisdiction specific data, the percentage of staff older than 54 years grew in 69% of administrations (see Figure 9.7).

Length of service

The difference in age profiles is also largely reflected in the length of service of tax administration staff. Figure 9.8. indicates that a significant number of administrations will not only face a large number of staff retiring over the next years, but that many of these staff will be very experienced, thus raising further issues about retention of key knowledge and experience.

Figure 9.6. Age profiles of tax administration staff, 2020

Percentage of staff by age bands for selected regional groupings

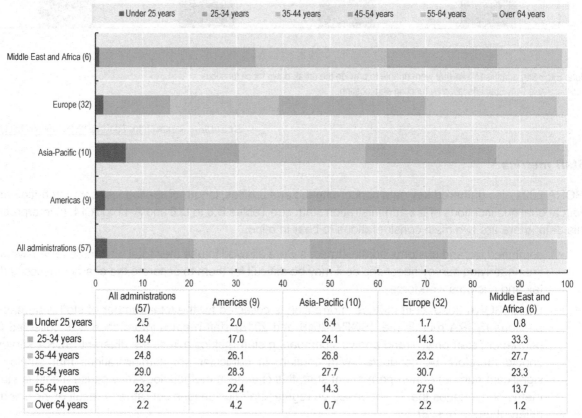

	All administrations (57)	Americas (9)	Asia-Pacific (10)	Europe (32)	Middle East and Africa (6)
■ Under 25 years	2.5	2.0	6.4	1.7	0.8
■ 25-34 years	18.4	17.0	24.1	14.3	33.3
■ 35-44 years	24.8	26.1	26.8	23.2	27.7
■ 45-54 years	29.0	28.3	27.7	30.7	23.3
■ 55-64 years	23.2	22.4	14.3	27.9	13.7
▢ Over 64 years	2.2	4.2	0.7	2.2	1.2

Percent

Note: The following administrations are included in the regional groupings: Americas (9) – Argentina, Brazil, Canada, Chile, Colombia, Costa Rica, Mexico, Peru and the United States; Asia-Pacific (10) – Australia, China (People's Republic of), Hong Kong, China, Indonesia, Japan, Korea, Malaysia, New Zealand, Singapore and Thailand; Europe (32) – Austria, Belgium, Bulgaria, Croatia, Cyprus, the Czech Republic, Denmark, Estonia, Finland, France, Georgia, Germany, Greece, Hungary, Iceland, Ireland, Italy, Latvia, Lithuania, Luxembourg, Malta, the Netherlands, Norway, Poland, Portugal, Romania, the Slovak Republic, Slovenia, Spain, Sweden, Switzerland and the United Kingdom; Middle East and Africa (6): Israel, Kenya, Morocco, Saudi Arabia, South Africa and Turkey.
Source: Table D.6 Staff age distribution.

StatLink ▨▧▧ https://doi.org/10.1787/888934311183

Figure 9.7. Staff older than 54 years: Movement between 2018 and 2020

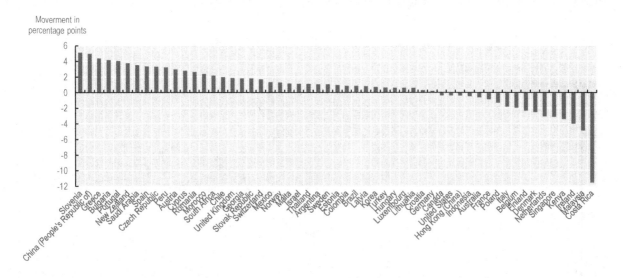

Note: Only includes jurisdictions for which data was available for both years. Data for Iceland has been excluded due to the merger of the Directorate of Internal Revenue and the Directorate of Customs on 1 January 2020.
Source: Table D.6 Staff age distribution.

StatLink ⬛🔢 https://doi.org/10.1787/888934311202

Figure 9.8. Average length of service vs. average age profile, 2020

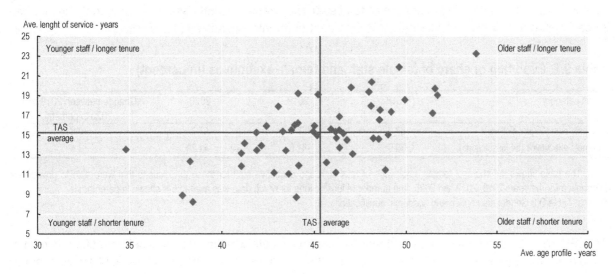

Source: OECD Secretariat calculations based on Tables D.6 Staff age distribution and D.7 Length of service.

StatLink ⬛🔢 https://doi.org/10.1787/888934311221

Gender distribution

In light of the strong public interest in gender equality, administrations were invited to report total staff and executive staff respectively by gender. As can be seen in Figure 9.9, while many administrations are close to the proportional line, typically female staff remains proportionally underrepresented in executive positions and significantly underrepresented (red oval) in a number of administrations, something that has remained unchanged since the 2017 edition of this report (OECD, 2017[2]).

Figure 9.9. Percentage of female staff – total female staff vs. female executives, 2020

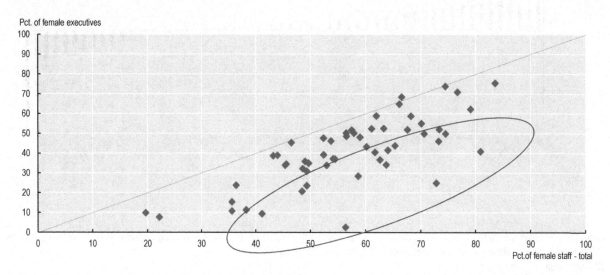

Source: Table D.8 Gender distribution and academic qualifications.

StatLink 🔊📊 https://doi.org/10.1787/888934311240

Looking at the overall averages, whilst there are variations between jurisdictions (see Table D.8), on average the share of female employees of total staff and executive staff has remained largely unchanged since 2018, with a very small increase of 3.4 percent of female executives (see Table 9.2).

Table 9.2. Evolution of share of female staff and female executives (in percent)

Staff category	2018	2019	2020	Change between 2018 and 2020 in percent
Female staff (56 jurisdictions)	57.3	57.9	57.7	+0.8
Female executives (54 jurisdictions)	39.9	41.6	41.2	+3.4

Note: The table shows the share of female employees of total staff and executive staff for those jurisdictions that were able to provide the information for the years 2018, 2019 and 2020. The number of jurisdictions for which data was available is shown in parenthesis.
Source: Table D.8 Gender distribution and academic qualifications.

The ISORA 2021 survey also asked administrations to indicate whether staff has self-identified as neither female nor male (referred to as "other" gender for the purposes of the survey). Table A.14 shows that two administrations, Australia and New Zealand, reported having staff who self-identified as "other".

Staff attrition

Staff attrition, also called staff turnover, refers to the rate at which employees leave an organisation during a defined period (normally a year). High attrition rates may result from a variety of factors, such as downsizing policies, demographics or changing staff preferences. The attrition rate should be considered together with other measures, such as the hire rate, which looks at the number of staff recruited during a defined period, when evaluating the human resource trends of an administration.

While a high attrition rate combined with a low hire rate is usually associated with a general downsizing policy – and may therefore be accepted – administrations should be concerned where both rates are high. Recruitment is costly, not only the recruitment process itself but also the cost and time for training and supporting new staff members, and the significant down time before new staff are fully operational or able to perform at the highest level. Having high attritions rates are generally to be avoided.

Having attrition rates that are too low may also not be ideal. While an organisation is growing, a low attrition rate may be accepted. However, in situations where both the attrition rate and the hire rate are low, an organisation may not have the ability to recruit new skills as all positions are filled. This could be an issue particularly for administrations that are undergoing transformation and therefore are in need of staff with skills that are different from what is currently available within the administration.

While what is considered a "healthy" attrition rate differs between industry sectors or jurisdictions, the average attrition rate for administrations participating in this publication of 6.0% in 2020 and the average hire rate of 6.1% in 2020 would seem to present a reasonable range for tax administrations of between 5% and 10%. It is worth noting that the average attrition and hire rates for 2020 are below those reported in previous years, which may be a pandemic related impact. It will be interesting to observe this trend in future editions of this series (see Table 9.3).

Table 9.3. Evolution of attrition and hire rates (in percent)

	2018	2019	2020	Change between 2018 and 2020 in percent
Attrition rates (51 jurisdictions)	6.8	7.3	6.0	-11.1
Hire rates (51 jurisdictions)	7.2	7.3	6.1	-15.7

Note: The table shows the average attrition and hire rates for those jurisdictions that were able to provide the information for the years 2018, 2019 and 2020. The number of jurisdictions for which data was available is shown in parenthesis. Data for China (People's Republic of), Iceland and Norway were excluded from the calculation as the result of extraordinary staff transfers over the period 2018 to 2020 which were recorded as recruitments, thus distorting their averages for those years (see notes in Table A.10.).
Source: Table D.5 Staff dynamics.

However, when looking at specific administration data, it becomes apparent that "attrition and hire" rates cover a very broad range. Figure 9.10 shows the relationship between tax administration attrition and hire rates. It illustrates that there are a number of administrations with attrition and hire rates well above 10% (upper-right box), while others show very low attrition and hire rates (lower-left box).

Figure 9.10. Attrition and hire rates, 2020

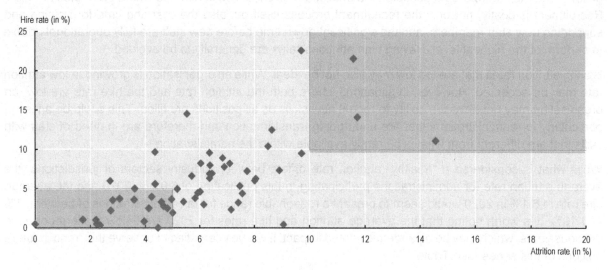

Note: Attrition rate = number of staff departures/average staffing level. Hire rate = number of staff recruitments/ average staffing level. The average staffing level equals opening staff numbers + end-of-year staff numbers/2.
Source: Table D.5 Staff dynamics.

StatLink https://doi.org/10.1787/888934311259

Whilst recruitment rates may vary by year, the challenge of training and knowledge transfer are constant. The COVID-19 pandemic brought these perennial issues into sharp focus as recruitment, and other on-boarding processes previously relied on face to face contact. As a result, new practices were developed quickly to complete these processes remotely. Tax administrations report that these practices brought benefits to the administration and candidates, and as a result they are now being adapted for the longer term.

Box 9.3. Examples – Enhancing recruitment processes

China (People's Republic of) – Digitising recruitment

The State Tax Administration (STA) has digitised civil servant recruitment processes to greatly improving efficiency. This has involved:

- STA accurately formulating recruitment planning and business requirements using data analysis.

- An online system to facilitate recruitment and registration. Using the examination and recruitment of civil servant management system, more than 700 000 candidates completed filling of personal information such as identity, education and experience. This meant that there could be a simultaneously completed online review of application qualifications and feedback of results within a week.

- Management software to promote recruitment interviews. Interview management software integrates candidate information, random allocation of interviewer and examination rooms, on-site lottery of examiners and candidates, automatic sorting of interview groups, real-time upload of interview scores and rapid generation of interview results. As a result approximately 50 000 candidates were interviewed within 3 to 4 days. Additionally video interviews were used during the COVID-19 epidemic to ensure a level playing field for candidates in severely affected areas.

Singapore - Digital transformation of HR processes

The Inland Revenue Authority of Singapore (IRAS) continues to harness technology and innovation to build greater organisational agility and a smarter digital workplace. For recruitment, IRAS uses artificial intelligence (AI) enabled conversational chatbots to handle and enhance applicants' experiences e.g. 24/7 access to complete the interview process and upload their resumes in one sitting. IRAS designed the conversation flow and questions harnessing AI, and the chatbots are also able to answer common queries on recruitment. IRAS customer satisfaction scores averaged 94% across job roles.

For ICT job roles, a chatbot with a technical test on programming languages provides automated AI scoring based on quality of codes, turnaround time and number of attempts for each applicant. IRAS has also incorporated verification features as the technical tests are completed off-site. At the outset, IRAS designed the chatbot work process to replace some manual processes, improving overall processing time.

There are other AI-powered tools that IRAS is developing. One tool seeks to match resumes of potential applicants with the job advertisements based on skills requirements, while another tool that is in development seeks to pilot a more competency-based assessment of job applicants. Just as importantly, IRAS has automated the traditional on-boarding process for new recruits that leverages data to initiate robotic process automation (RPA) tasks for mass auto-creation of staff accounts. There are resultant efficiencies in relation to notifying and providing relevant information to the parties involved to perform their tasks, benefitting both new recruits and the HR team.

Sources: China (People's Republic of) (2022) and Singapore (2022).

Supporting staff

The changes tax administrations are managing, whether technology, policy or budget driven, are significant. In addition, the wider digitalistion of the economy is changing the service expectations of taxpayers, and staff need the right tools and support to adapt. As a result, tax administrations are considering the best way to support staff through these changes, ensuring they have the right tools for the tasks. Changes to the workplace also mean that established practices around performance management are being adapted based on the learning gained from the rapid switch to digital channels in the COVID-19 pandemic.

As a result, tax administrations are reporting that they are investing in services that can help 'frontline' staff better understand taxpayers needs, and provide better services to them. This can cover a range of channels from call centres through to social media. These investments are allowing tax administrations to provide improved services, and their staff feel better equipped to deliver those high quality services. Tax administrations also report that sophisticated analytics are being used to match staff skills to taxpayer needs.

Box 9.4. Examples – Supporting staff

Canada - Empathy in Service

Canada Revenue Agency (CRA) research has shown that negative interactions with clients can have significant impacts on voluntary compliance. Using empathy to guide the design, delivery and support of the agency's services, reduces the negative emotions that clients can have from interactions with the CRA. The CRA has launched two national awareness campaigns to provide employees with

---

information, tools, and resources to help implement the CRA's vision of being trusted, fair and helpful by putting people first. The first Empathy in Service campaign was launched across the Agency in October 2020 and provided employees with tools to apply empathy in their work. An Empathy Working Group made up of employees supported the campaign. The success of this initiative led to the development of the 'Spotlight on Service' Initiative, a month long campaign to reinforce service concepts with employees, focusing on accessibility, diversity and inclusion, and putting people first both from an internal and external service perspective. As a result:

- 71% of employees agree that all CRA activities are supported by a culture of service excellence.
- 87% of employees agree that all employees, regardless of the role they play in the organization, contribute to CRA's culture of service excellence.
- 98% of employees agree that they understand the importance of using empathy at work with colleagues and clients.

China (People's Republic of) – Improving performance management

In 2021, the State Taxation Administration (STA) optimised and upgraded the "e-personnel management system", by connecting individual performance management with organizational performance management. This enabled STA to encourage tax officials to better perform their responsibilities and improve their work efficiency and capability. This included:

- Tailored evaluation. Based on each tax official's responsibilities, the organisational performance tasks, annual key tasks and individual tasks are set for each tax official in the form of individual performance indicators.
- Standardised cycles. The implementation, evaluation and feedback of performance management are deeply integrated with the processes of daily assessment of individual performance to form an integrated assessment and evaluation system.
- Applied results. The results of performance evaluation are applied to the selection, appointment, promotion, education and training of tax officials. This promotes a better work atmosphere of being willing and able to get work done well.
- Upgraded system. As the information for performance evaluations is collected in a one-stop shop the e-personnel management system has been upgraded to realise the digitalisation of the whole process of individual performance management.

United Kingdom - Analysis to identify taxpayer service needs and trends

The roll out of the United Kingdom's (UK) Her Majesty's Revenue and Customs (HMRC) digital services has led to a corresponding growth in information about customers' experiences and feedback on these services. This provides valuable data for customer insight, which HMRC can use to improve customer experience and make future innovations in services. As the range of channels and customer interactions increase, HMRC want to understand how customer experience across different 'contact points' impacts customers to make their experience as effortless as possible, whilst also ensuring tax compliance.

The growth in customer data presents several challenges. Together with the sheer volumes, the increasingly unstructured nature of customer data means that traditional tools are ill-suited for drawing timely and actionable insights. Customer feedback varies from the generic to highly specific. For example, customers often use different words to describe the same experiences and the sentiment within their responses can be difficult to decipher. HMRC therefore use a combination of proprietary software and in-house models to gain efficient and deeper understanding of the data. Based on powerful algorithms and machine learning principles, the tools help make sense of customer experience across channels, rapidly sorting and categorising the information to generate a usable taxonomy of themes and issues.

Over the past 18 months, HMRC have analysed several million pieces of customer feedback and engagement, building a view of customer experience and emerging trends across HMRC digital services, telephony, and social media. In turn, this information has helped generate valuable insights, informing management of the impacts of existing HMRC services, such as those focused on the UK Self-Assessment filing process, as well as of potential future enhancements of customer support services.

Sources: Canada (2022), China (People's Republic of) (2022) and the United Kingdom (2022).

Anecdotal evidence, gathered through numerous Forum on Tax Administration (FTA) meetings, shows that tax administrations put considerable efforts into supporting staff during periods of transition, including through the COVID-19 crisis, considering issues such as:

- **Staff welfare**, which includes looking into staff motivation and satisfaction, health and safety related issues, work-life balance, assistance programmes, and ergonomic office equipment; and
- **Staff training**, which includes how to best support those that have been given new tasks, those that have to perform their tasks from home instead of the office, as well as those that are leading partially or wholly virtual teams for the first time.

As tax administrations consider the post pandemic workplace, these issues will continue to be of high priority. The experience gained during the pandemic will be highly useful in shaping the new ways of working.

Technology is also providing new opportunities to analyse existing processes to look for efficiencies, including throught the use of artificial intelligence and machine learning to automate some of the core tasks within a tax administration. Chapter 6 (Table 6.1) highlights the rapid growth in the use of such services with for example, more than 50% of administrations reporting that they now using or planning to use robotic process automation (see also Figure 9.11 for the up-take of RPA by tax administrations). This is helping tax administrations respond to budgetary and workforce pressures as it is freeing up resource for staff to be focussed on more complex tasks.

Figure 9.11. Evolution of the implementation and use of Robotic Process Automation, 2018 to 2020

Percent of administrations

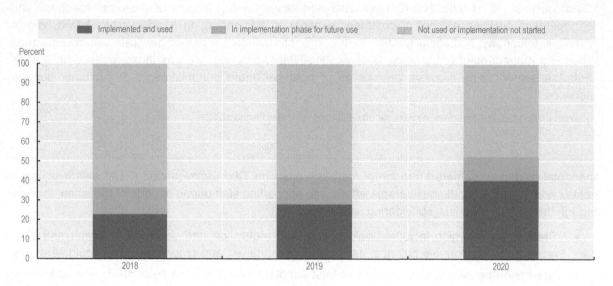

Source: Table A.52 Innovative technologies: Implementation and usage (Part 2).

StatLink ⟦ᵐˢᴸ⟧ https://doi.org/10.1787/888934311278

Box 9.5. Examples - Automation in tax administration

Australia - Robotic Process Automation

The Australian Taxation Office (ATO uses robotic process automation (RPA) in conjunction with process optimisation techniques to remove unnecessary steps from the audit process and to automate repetitive manual processing steps. This enables auditors to increase the time which they spend applying judgement to the facts of audit cases. Using automation software the ATO have been able to:

- ensure cases are created and delivered directly to a staff member – rather than have team leaders allocate work

- provide staff with a consistent and relevant profile of each client attached to each case for quick and easy reference

- close cases automatically.

This has so far reduced time spent on manual actions by 5%, and has allowed staff to understand the needs of taxpayers more easily and ensure appropriate empathy upon engagement as they can focus on what matters most in every interaction with taxpayers.

Canada - Robotic Process Automation

The Canada Revenue Agency (CRA) vision of the future of work is meaningful work that is engaging and rewarding for employees on a daily basis. RPA has a significant role in this as it can take the repetitive processes out of the work, and improve the day-to-day tasks of CRA employees by automating high volume, highly repetitive administrative tasks, that are prone to human error. To date, the CRA has automated 8 processes, saving more than 34 000 staff hours, the equivalent of approximately 25 additional full-time CRA employees. The process automations launched in CRA range

---

from screening suspicious accounts for fraudulent risk, to transferring unallocated payments from taxpayers, and assisting with scheduling Contact Centre employees. These activities would traditionally have been completed by employees and through automation, these employees now have the ability to focus on more value added tasks and their higher priority deliverables.

As a result of these process automations, employees have reported increased job satisfaction subsequent to the removal of monotonous tasks, as well as an improved ability to focus on more value-added work. Benefits realized also include improved data quality, increased productivity, as well as enhanced compliance and decreased operational risk. Most process automations can progress from feasibility to production within 8-16 weeks, or faster for high priority low/complexity initiatives. The CRA continues to identify additional opportunities for automation in the future.

Israel - Robotic Process Automation

RPA aims to mimic user actions, such as logging into different systems and extracting data. This innovative process is designed to replace the manual work of an employee who performs repetitive technical work, on a large number of cases without the need to exercise discretion.

For the purpose of testing and operating RPA, the Israel Tax Authority (ITA) was looking for a suitable work process and identified a unit that inspects taxpayers working in two or more workplaces who did not adjust their tax liability to account for multiple employers. When there is a tax liability according to the data, the unit's employees send a recommendation to the tax office to reach out to the taxpayer. RPA was programmed to perform the employee's work by learning the exact work process of the employees. RPA was programmed to produce the same data as the employee would have (such as: salaries, withholding tax, credits, deductions, etc.). The RPA software then enters the data generated into the tax simulator system in order to calculate the taxpayer's potential tax liability. After the programming was completed, tests were performed on the work results. A large number of cases were taken as a sample, and the comparison showed that RPA's results were similar to the employees results. The test also identified that the average time per case saved is 97% and 99.6% saving in cost. As a result of the test the ITA is investing further in RPA.

See Annex 9.A for supporting material.

Netherlands - Robotic Process Automation

The Netherlands Tax Administration (NTA) has many repetitive but essential tasks that do not make work attractive for employees. To address this, the NTA started investigating RPA, and identified invoice processing (paying suppliers) as a suitable start. The RPA-project was consciously kept small, aiming to solely robotise this first step, with the aim of eventually moving to full e-invoicing.

The aims of the project were to improve the quality of work for employees on one hand and on the other improving quality of the invoicing process by minimising errors and failures, so that legal requirements on payment terms could be met.

The outcomes surpassed expectations as employees experienced time savings of four hours per day which gave them space to deal with more productive tasks such as service quality improvements and knowledge development.

See Annex 9.A for supporting material.

Norway – Artificial Intelligence

The Norwegian Tax Administration (NTA) has a strategic initiative for scaling the capacity to develop and administer AI models, such as.

- Machine learning model for simple processing of compensation applications. The NTA is responsible for the administration of compensation schemes for businesses and self-employed persons during COVID-19, under which eligible taxpayers could apply for compensation for the loss of income. The number of applications was greater than the NTA's capacity for manual case processing, so a machine-learning model was created that recognised applications that would have been approved anyway, making manual case processing unnecessary. This saves approximately one day's work per application, which ensures an acceptable case processing time.

- Synthetic test population for the National Population Register. The National Population Register is a national common component with an overview of all persons living in or connected to Norway. The National Population Register has automated processes for collecting and distributing information. External users of the National Population Register need to test their systems in a way that ensures privacy protection. To achieve this, they need event-driven test data. The NTA has used machine learning to create dynamic and synthetic test data, as well as a test generator that simulates various events in the National Population Register that can be used by all National Population Register users.

Sweden - Use of machine translation

The Swedish Tax Agency's machine translation service was first implemented in June 2020 and was initially used by staff working with an EU directive (DAC6). In November 2021, the service was made available to all staff. Since then, it has been used to translate over 730 000 documents: an average of about 200 documents a day.

The service supports translation from 33 languages and is mainly used to translate incoming communications to Swedish. Tax administrators can gain a quick overview of what a document is about, which helps them to decide whether or not all or part of it needs to be sent to an authorised translator. All data is processed strictly within the Swedish Tax Agency's infrastructure, which means that the service can be used to translate sensitive information.

The key benefits of the service include:

- offering a better understanding of communications from individuals and businesses
- savings on translation costs
- secure personal data processing
- faster communication response times

The machine translation service is based on an open-source neural translation model that has been trained on large volumes of texts translated by humans. It learns from this input and can then translate new texts in a similar way. The model and training texts have been provided by the Department of Digital Humanities at the University of Helsinki (Tiedemann and Thottingal, 2020[3]). A large proportion of the training texts used were official EU materials in different EU languages.

United States - Robotic Process Automation

The Internal Revenue Service (IRS) is advancing the application of data and analytics to operations through the use of intelligent automation (IA). Two recent use cases are:

- Determining the ongoing suitability of third-party payroll administrators requires extensive financial compliance checks on the administrator and any related businesses and individuals. Due to time and resource constraints, the programme was only able to check 20% of the related businesses for compliance annually and was heavily burdened by repeated checks when non-compliance was found. To alleviate the resource constraint, IA was used to automate research in a mainframe application and record results in a formatted report for review by programme staff. The automation reduced the time to conduct a check from 60 minutes to roughly 10-15 minutes in preliminary performance testing and is expected to increase the capacity of the program to check 100% of related businesses quarterly. The automation also collects and summarises key data points to help inform suspension decisions for payroll administrators.

- Historically, prioritisation of non-filer cases was done using a simple method of ordering on largest assessment value. By analysing over 60 thousand historical business returns, the automation used machine learning to identify potentially productive and unproductive inventory based on the return's attributes. This research-based prioritisation approach was shown to boost desired outcomes by approx. 14% when compared to prioritising based on largest assessment value. Based on the model's demonstrated accuracy and precision rates, this prioritisation approach is estimated to yield an additional approx. USD 7.5 million per year across around 1 400 potential assessments.

Sources: Australia (2022), Canada (2022), Israel (2022), Netherlands (2022) Norway (2022), Sweden (2022) and the United States (2022).

Developing staff capability

While ISORA 2021 did not survey administrations as regards their strategy and approaches towards increasing staff capability, this remains a key topic for all administrations. This report highlights many areas of change that are taking place within administrations, and effective change relies on the capabilities of staff being developed. This is particularly important with digital transformation, as this frequently requires new skill sets. The OECD Digital Transformation Maturity Model contains a section on skills development and workforce planning, and is useful tool for administrations identifying the skills they need (OECD, 2021[4]). Figures 9.12 and 9.13 highlight how tax administrations are preparing the ground for digital transformation by mapping the skills needed for digital transformation, and investing in staff training to build capability. Also of note is the collaborative approaches highlighted in Figure 9.13, reflective of the wide impacts that digital transformation brings, and the need for shared approaches.

162 |

Figure 9.12. Skills for digital transformation: Identification and mapping, 2022

Percent of administrations

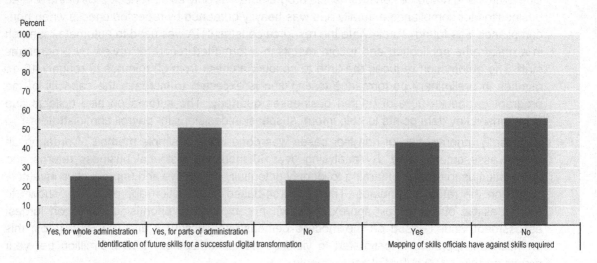

Note: The figure is based on ITTI data from 52 jurisdictions that are covered in this report and that have completed the global survey on digitalisation.
Source: OECD et al. (2022), Inventory of Tax Technology Initiatives, https://www.oecd.org/tax/forum-on-tax-administration/tax-technology-tools-and-digital-solutions/, Table SG3 (accessed on 13 May 2022).

StatLink https://doi.org/10.1787/888934311297

Figure 9.13. Skills for digital transformation: Collaboration with government organisations or external partners, 2022

Percent of administrations

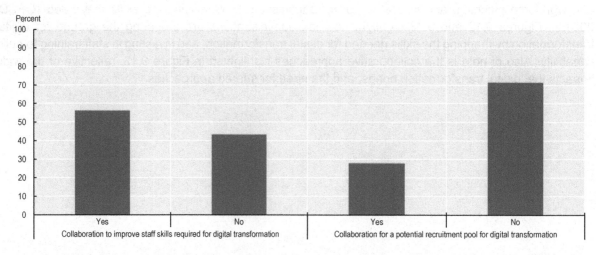

Note: The figure shows those administrations that have identified the future skills needed for a successful digital transformation either for the whole administrations or for parts of it (see Figure 9.12.). It is based on ITTI data from 52 jurisdictions that are covered in this report and that have completed the global survey on digitalisation.
Source: OECD et al. (2022), Inventory of Tax Technology Initiatives, https://www.oecd.org/tax/forum-on-tax-administration/tax-technology-tools-and-digital-solutions/, Table SG3 (accessed on 13 May 2022).

StatLink https://doi.org/10.1787/888934311316

In parallel, one of the challenges of remote or hybrid working arrangements is maintaining staff training, and as a result administrations have been reconsidering their approaches to delivering general training. Tax administrations report moving their training programmes into a virtual environment, using live online training sessions or pre-recorded videos/webinars.

While moving to a virtual training environment may have some up-front costs, it may save costs in the longer term as once produced, pre-recorded training material can be viewed at any time, from anywhere. Remote training can reduce travel expenses and can allow staff to learn at their own pace and convenience as well as increasing the number of staff members that can follow a course. New technologies are also helping facilitate the collaborative learning aspects, increasing the quality of the training experience.

Box 9.6. Examples – Staff development

Canada - Empowering a hybrid workplace

As part of the move to hybrid working, the CRA has enabled cloud-based technologies that have transformed the use of secure virtual collaboration platforms for meetings, town halls, recruitment, and distance learning. The CRA has equipped its employees with tools to support an accessible and inclusive virtual workplace. New technologies to enable collaboration continue to be explored and deployed.

Additionally, the CRA has used advanced analytics to create a prediction model for retirements to support talent management and staffing plans; and, used AI to analyse text data from employee surveys during the pandemic, to ensure the Agency has the best possible understanding of its workforce for decision making. Going forward, the CRA will be applying these techniques and others to help understand employee movement in the organisation as well new approaches to leadership in a hybrid model of working.

Portugal - Rethinking training and learning for the future workforce demands

AT has promoted online training actions, webinars and workshops more adapted to the circumstances of remote work, addressing subjects like leadership, time management and communication skills. It has also developed training in the behavioural and social aspects of remote work, such as mindfulness or time management skills.

One of the challenges has been that not all functions can be performed remotely such as border control, tax and customs inspection (external) and procedures and processes related to tax justice in administrative and tax courts. Therefore, several strategies have been implemented to progress to a digital work place and to allow a better compatibility of remote / face-to-face work (hybrid model).

Other measures are also planned such as changing the human resources competencies model so skills needs align with the wider AT work strategy. This will help ensure that future roles will have the required skills clearly identified. AT is working on training programmes to meet such demands.

Sweden - Leadership development programme

The Swedish Tax Agency (STA) has high ambitions for increasing its capacity to respond to the demands of change and development. In a rapidly changing world, leaders need to be adaptable in terms of the way they act and collaborate, and the Human Resources Department needs to support them in more flexible and agile ways.

To support this, in 2021, the STA ran a series of leadership summits for executive management. The topics covered included collaborative approaches to developing the corporate culture and promoting positive leadership behaviours.

To bring about meaningful change, the STA plans to involve all managers – including leaders without staff responsibility – in improving abilities in several areas. These include interaction between and within different levels of the organisation; decision-making; and agility.

HR is in the process of establishing a flexible new range of courses and training opportunities that will help to strengthen leadership, improve self-awareness, and challenge behaviours. HR aims to create mixed groups, including leaders and managers from different departments with varying levels of experience. HR plans to offer this training to all the leaders, with the ambition to match leaders with similar competence needs.

Sources: Canada (2022), Portugal (2022) and Sweden (2022).

Note

[1] Previous editions reported the allocation of staff resources across seven functional groupings: (i) Registration and taxpayer services; (ii) Returns and payment processing; (iii) Audit, investigation and other verification; (iv) Debt collection; (v) Dispute and appeals; (vi) Information and communication technology; and (vii) Other functions. Starting with ISORA 2020 those seven groupings were reduced to the four groupings shown in Figure 9.5.

References

OECD (2021), *Digital Transformation Maturity Model*, OECD, Paris, https://www.oecd.org/tax/forum-on-tax-administration/publications-and-products/digital-transformation-maturity-model.htm (accessed on 13 May 2022). [4]

OECD (2021), *Towards sustainable remote working in a post COVID-19 environment*, https://www.oecd.org/coronavirus/policy-responses/tax-administration-towards-sustainable-remote-working-in-a-post-covid-19-environment-fdc0844d/. [1]

OECD (2017), *Tax Administration 2017: Comparative Information on OECD and Other Advanced and Emerging Economies*, OECD Publishing, Paris, https://doi.org/10.1787/tax_admin-2017-en. [2]

Tiedemann, J. and S. Thottingal (2020), *OPUS-MT – Building open translation services for the World*, European Association for Machine Translation, https://aclanthology.org/2020.eamt-1.61 (accessed on 13 May 2022). [3]

Annex 9.A. Links to supporting material (accessed on 13 May 2022)

- Box 9.1. – Chile: Link to a video that provides more information on the mobility plan: https://www.youtube.com/watch?v=HM_-sHc310Q
- Box 9.5. – Israel: Link to a presentation with more detail on the results of the automation project: https://www.oecd.org/tax/forum-on-tax-administration/database/b.9.5-israel-using-rpa-technology-in-the-ita.pdf
- Box 9.5. – Netherlands: Link to a factsheet on robotic process automation at the Netherlands Tax Administration: https://www.oecd.org/tax/forum-on-tax-administration/database/b.9.5-netherlands-factsheet-rpa.pdf

Made in United States
North Haven, CT
03 December 2024

61637764R00096